WORDLY WISE 3000®
THIRD EDITION

BOOK 7

Systematic Academic Vocabulary Development

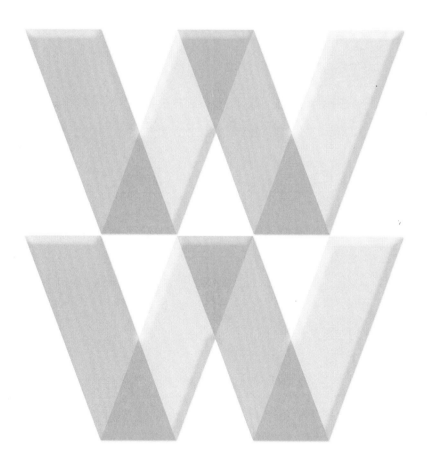

Kenneth Hodkinson | Sandra Adams

School Specialty, Inc.
Cambridge and Toronto

Editorial Project Manager: Kate Moltz
Senior Editor: Will Tripp
Editor: Rachel Smith
Senior Designer: Deborah Rodman
Cover Design: Michelle Mohnkern

Illustration Credits:
Lessons 2, 14, 17, 18: Q2AMedia.

Photograph Credits: Lesson 1: Robfergusonjr; Lesson 3: Andreagrossmann; Lesson 4: Charles Kaye/ Fotolia; Lesson 5: HC/Fotolia; Lesson 6: Christopher Walker/Fotolia; Lesson 7: Durova; Lesson 8: Library of Congress Prints and Photographs Division Washington, D.C. 20540 USA; Lesson 9: Robot Michiel; Lesson 10: Nicolas Larento/Fotolia; Lesson 11: Philippe Kurlapski; Lesson 12: Leeds City Art Gallery; Lesson 13: Library of Congress Prints and Photographs Division Washington, D.C. 20540 USA; Lesson 15: David Sytsma/Fotolia; Lesson 16: Richard McGuirk/Fotolia; Lesson 19: Beatrice Preve/Fotolia; Lesson 20: Masterfile.

Printed in Benton Harbor, MI, in May 2017
ISBN 978-0-8388-7607-7

14 15 PPG 19 18 17

Contents

Welcome to *Wordly Wise 3000®*

You've been learning words since you were a tiny baby. At first, you learned them only by hearing other people talk. Now that you are a reader, you have another way to learn words.

Obviously, it's important to know what words mean, but lots of times, we think we can get away without knowing some of them as we read. This could cause a problem. Say you are reading the directions for a new game. You know most of the words in the sentence you're reading. Then you stop for a word you don't recognize:

> *Please do not touch the* blegmy *or your score will be lost.*

You ask yourself, "What is a *blegmy?*" At first you think, "Well, it's only one word." But then you think, "What is it that I'm not supposed to touch?" All of a sudden, knowing what that one word means is important!

Clearly, the more words you know, the better your understanding of everything you read. *Wordly Wise 3000* will help you learn a lot of words, but it can't teach you *all* the words you'll ever need. It can, however, help guide your learning of new words on your own.

How Do You Learn What Words Mean?

There are two main ways you learn what words mean: directly and indirectly.

You have to learn some words *directly*. You may study them for a class, look them up in a dictionary or glossary, or ask someone what they mean. You also learn word meanings *indirectly* by hearing and reading the words. In fact, the more you listen and read, the more words you'll learn. Reading books, magazines, and online can help build your vocabulary.

At school, you learn a lot of words directly. If you're using this book, you are learning words directly. You are reading the words, learning what they mean, and studying them. Then you are practicing them as you do the activities. Finally, you might even use them in your own writing or conversations. There is an old saying: "Use a word three times and it's yours." Three times might not be enough, of course, but the idea is right. The more you practice using a word, the better you understand it.

What Is "School Language"?

School language—or school words—are the words you find in the books you read, from novels to textbooks, and on tests. You read them online as you look up information. Your teacher uses these words to explain an important concept about math or reading. Some have to do with a particular topic, such as the building of the Great Pyramid in Egypt. Others are words for tasks you are being asked to do, such as *summarize*. These words are different from the kinds of words you use when you're hanging out with your friends or talking casually with your family. That's why you often need to study these words directly.

Wordly Wise 3000 is designed to teach you some of the words you need to do well in school and on tests—and later on in your jobs. It will also help you learn how to learn more words. Remember, there is no single thing that will help you understand what you read as much as knowing word meanings will.

How Do You Figure Out Word Meanings?

What should you do when you come to a word and you think you don't know what it means?

Say It
First, say it to yourself. Maybe once you do this, it will sound like a word you *do* know. Sometimes you know a word in your head without knowing what it looks like in print. So if you match up what you know and what you read—you have the word!

Use Context
If this doesn't work, take the next step: look at the context of the word— the other words and sentences around it. Sometimes these can give you a clue to the word's meaning. Here's an example:

Mr. Huerta had great respect for his opponent.

Say that you don't know what *opponent* means. Does Mr. Huerta have respect for his teacher? His mother? Then you read on:

The two players sat across from each other in the warm room. The chessboard was between them. Both looked as if they were concentrating very hard.

Now you see that Mr. Huerta is taking part in a chess game. You know that in a chess game, one person plays another. So his *opponent* must be the person he is playing against. You reread the sentence using that meaning. Yes, that works. In this sentence, *opponent* means "someone you play against, or compete with."

Use Word Parts

If the context doesn't help, look at the parts of the word. Does it have any prefixes you know? How about suffixes? Or roots? These can help you figure out what it means. Look at this sentence:

Shania had the misfortune *to hurt her arm right before the swim meet.*

If you don't know the meaning of *misfortune*, try looking at parts of the word. You might know that *fortune* means "luck." Maybe *mis-* is a prefix. You could look it up, or maybe you remember its meaning from studying prefixes in school. The prefix *mis-* means a few different things, but one of them is "bad." You try it out and reread the sentence using that meaning. It would certainly be bad luck, or a *misfortune,* to hurt your arm before a swim meet.

Look It Up

If saying the word or using context and word parts don't work, you can look it up in a dictionary—either a book or online reference—or a glossary.

Nobody knows the meaning of every word, but good readers know how to use these strategies to figure out words they don't know. Get into the habit of using them as you read, and you may be surprised at how automatic it becomes!

How Well Do You Know a Word?

It's important to know many words and to keep on learning more. But it's also important to know them well. In fact, some experts say that there are four levels of knowing a word:

1. I never saw/heard it before.
2. I've heard/seen it, but I don't know what it means.
3. I think it has something to do with…
4. I know it.*

Just because you can read a word and have memorized its definition, it doesn't mean that you know that word well. You want to know it so well that you know when to use it and when to use another word instead. One way to help deepen your knowledge of a word is to use a graphic organizer like the one below that tells about the word *portion*.

Concept of Definition Map

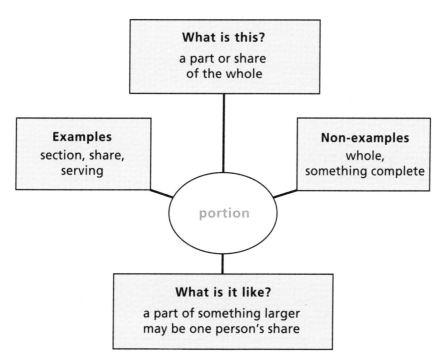

If you can fill in all the parts of this graphic organizer, you are well on your way to really knowing the word *portion*.

*Dale, E., & O'Rourke, J. (1986). *Vocabulary Building*. Columbus, OH: Zaner-Bloser.

Did you know you can access *Wordly Wise 3000* online?

Go to www.WordlyWise3000.com and you will find:

Word Lists for all the lessons

The Word Lists allow you to read the words and their definitions and listen to how they are pronounced.

The Word Lists can also be downloaded onto your MP3 player. You can download them and study them wherever you are—home, on the bus, in study period—a great use of your time.

A Quick Check question for every word

You can check your understanding of each word right away. That helps you know which words you need to spend more time studying.

Games for every book

Games are grouped to use as reviews, just as you would use the Review Puzzles in your book. Use them to practice and have fun with the words you've learned.

Good luck in your study of words. It takes some work, but it will pay off in the end.

For more practice and games, go to **www.WordlyWise3000.com**.

Word List	Study the definitions of the words. Then do the exercises that follow.

abate
ə bāt´

v. To become weaker; to decrease.
The speaker waited until the applause had **abated** before continuing.

unabated *adj.* Showing no sign of weakening; showing no decrease.
Representative Millet showed **unabated** enthusiasm for campaigning for the senate seat, even though he had been twice defeated for that office.

acknowledge
ak näl´ ij

v. 1. To admit the existence of.
Did the police officer **acknowledge** your right to remain silent?

2. To express recognition or thanks for.
The new Wimbledon singles champion raised her hand to **acknowledge** the cheers of the crowd.

acknowledged *adj.* Commonly accepted or recognized.
Bill James is an **acknowledged** expert on baseball statistics.

agent
ā´ jənt

n. 1. A person who acts or does business for another.
The author's **agent** found a company to publish his latest mystery story.

2. Something that brings about a result.
A new principal can be a powerful **agent** for change in a school.

authority
ə thôr´ ə tē

n. 1. The right to give orders, make decisions, or take action.
Only the Congress of the United States has the **authority** to declare war.

2. An expert source of information.
The researcher Jane Goodall is a world **authority** on chimpanzees.

authorities *n.* A group of people who have the right to enforce laws.
The **authorities** closed the restaurant because it did not meet the proper standards for cleanliness.

devastate
dev´ ə stāt

v. To ruin or destroy completely.
Farmers in the Midwest fear that lack of rain will **devastate** the wheat crop.

devastating *adj.* Causing destruction.
A **devastating** hurricane destroyed hundreds of homes in southern Florida.

devastation *n.* Great destruction.
The earthquake in Japan created a scene of massive **devastation.**

epidemic ep ə dem´ ik	*n.* The rapid spreading of a disease to many people at one time. The flu **epidemic** of 1918 killed over twenty million people in the Northern Hemisphere. *adj.* Spreading rapidly as a disease over a wide area. AIDS became **epidemic** in central Africa in the 1980s.
estimate es´ tə mət	*n.* A number that is not exact; a careful guess. The mechanic's **estimate** for repairing the car is $1000. *v.* (es´ tə māt) To figure out roughly; to make an approximate calculation. We **estimate** that it will take us an hour to drive to the airport.
evict ē vikt´	*v.* To force out of property by taking legal action. The landlord threatened to **evict** the tenants for not paying the rent.
impartial im pär´ shəl	*adj.* Not favoring one side more than another; fair. A judge should be **impartial** in the courtroom.
industrious in dus´ trē əs	*adj.* Hardworking; not lazy. The more **industrious** workers in the clothing factory were rewarded with pay raises at the end of the year.
infuriate in fyoor´ ē āt	*v.* To make very angry. Cruelty to animals **infuriates** me.
irrelevant ir rel´ ə vənt	*adj.* Having nothing to do with the subject. The candidate's personal wealth is **irrelevant** to our discussion about his qualifications for the job.
precise pri sīs´	*adj.* Exact; accurate. Do you know the **precise** time that your plane arrives? **precision** *n.* (pri sizh´ ən) Exactness. An eye surgeon's work requires great **precision.**
sham sham	*n.* Something fake or false. Their offer to make us rich turned out to be a **sham.** *adj.* Not genuine; fake. Although he tried to appear sorry, his **sham** apology fooled no one. *v.* To pretend. We **shammed** illness so we could stay home.
trek trek	*n.* A long, slow, and difficult journey. The hikers were exhausted after their **trek** over the mountain. *v.* To travel slowly and with difficulty. Sam **trekked** ten miles into town after his car broke down.

Choose two phrases to form a sentence that correctly uses a word from Word List 1. Write each sentence in the space provided.

1. (a) you make that person very angry. (c) If you infuriate someone,
   (b) you act in that person's place.   (d) If you evict someone,

   _C a_ _____

   _____

2. (a) something that is not genuine. (c) An estimate is
   (b) a decrease in size or amount.   (d) A sham is

   _d a_ _____

   _____

3. (a) a disease that spreads rapidly. (c) An epidemic is
   (b) a number that is not exact.   (d) An agent is

   _c a_ _____

   _____

4. (a) that is meant to be helpful.   (c) A devastating comment is one
   (b) An irrelevant comment is one   (d) that is off the subject.

   _b d_ _____

   _____

5. (a) An agent is   (c) something that cannot be explained.
   (b) A trek is   (d) something that produces a result.

   _a d_ _____

   _____

6. (a) one who works hard.   (c) An industrious person is
   (b) An impartial person is   (d) one who is highly paid.

   _c a_ _____

   _____

7. (a) Estimates are   (c) people who enforce the law.
   (b) Authorities are   (d) witnesses to an accident.

   _b c_ _____

   _____

8. (a) is strongly denied.   (c) Something that is acknowledged
   (b) is generally accepted.   (d) Something that is unabated

   _d b_ _____

   _____

9. (a) a state of destruction.　　　(c) Precision is
   (b) Devastation is　　　　　　　(d) a sticking or holding together.

   _b_ _a_ _____

   _____

10. (a) An authority is　　　　　　(c) an expert source of information.
    (b) a decrease in force or power.　(d) A trek is

    _a_ _c_ _____

    _____

    _____

1B ▷ Just the Right Word

Improve each of the following sentences by crossing out the bold phrase and replacing it with a word (or a form of the word) from Word List 1.

1. The people had no right to be there, so they were **removed by force** from the house.
   evicted

2. The governor has the **right under the law** to appoint judges to state courts.
   athoraty

3. Those called for jury duty are expected to be **fair and not to favor either side.**
   imparshal

4. The parts of a jigsaw puzzle must be cut with **very great care** if they are to fit together properly.
   presise

5. In a special ceremony, the town **expressed its gratitude for** the heroic act of the firefighter.
   acknowledged

6. To succeed in the movie business, you need a good **person to represent you.**
   agent

7. The carpenter will **give a rough idea of** the cost of building a deck.
   estimate

8. We waited for the traffic to **decrease in volume** before we left the city.
   abate

9. Yesterday's tornado in eastern Kansas **completely ruined** a trailer park.
   devistated

10. We **made a long and difficult journey** across the desert for three days.
    treked

Word List

abate
acknowledge
agent
authority
devastate
epidemic
estimate
evict
impartial
industrious
infuriate
irrelevant
precise
sham
trek

Circle the letter or letters of each correct answer. A question may have more than one correct answer.

1. Which of the following can be **shammed?**
   (a) concern
   (b) honesty
   (c) sleep
   (d) interest

2. Which of the following might be **estimated?**
   (a) the cost of repairs
   (b) the height of a hill
   (c) the population of a town
   (d) the number of days in a week

3. Which of the following would be **irrelevant** in judging a student's writing?
   (a) the student's age
   (b) the student's name
   (c) the width of the margins
   (d) the color of the ink used

4. Which of the following might result in someone's being **evicted** from a house?
   (a) failing to pay the rent
   (b) using it for illegal purposes
   (c) causing damage to it
   (d) running a business from it

5. Which of the following can **abate?**
   (a) anger
   (b) high winds
   (c) silence
   (d) applause

6. Which of the following are **precise** amounts?
   (a) 2,145
   (b) several hundred
   (c) half a dozen
   (d) a lot

7. Which of the following might be considered a **trek?**
   (a) a trip to the corner store
   (b) a ride in a hot-air balloon
   (c) a walk across Canada
   (d) a plane trip to Europe

8. Which of the following would be **devastating** to a town?
   (a) a new mayor
   (b) an earthquake
   (c) a shopping mall
   (d) a celebration

Circle the two synonyms in each group of words.

1. (authority   expert)   agent   practice
2. (admit   acknowledge)   forget   devastate
3. (calculation   decision   estimate)   trek
4. secret   irrelevant   (fair   impartial)
5. weak   (fake   precise   sham)
6. increase   (destroy   devastate)   infuriate

Circle the two antonyms in each group of words.

7. (abate   rule   increase)   evict
8. trek   deny   (infuriate   soothe)
9. epidemic   (precise   inaccurate)   angry
10. (industrious   irrelevant   strong   lazy)

abate
acknowledge
agent
authority
devastate
epidemic
estimate
evict
impartial
industrious
infuriate
irrelevant
precise
sham
trek

The Trail of Tears

The original inhabitants of what is now Kentucky and Tennessee were an **industrious** people who lived mainly by hunting and farming. They were called Cherokees by the Europeans who first made contact with them. The Europeans had settled along the East Coast in the early 1600s. These first meetings between European traders and Cherokees were friendly but were to have **devastating** consequences for the Native Americans later. The Europeans brought goods for trading, it's true. But they also brought smallpox, a disease that had been unknown in North America before their arrival. This disease left the body covered with sores and was often fatal. In 1745, a smallpox **epidemic** struck the Cherokee people. It killed more than half the population. And that was just the beginning of the Cherokee people's woes.

The United States government recognized the Cherokee Nation as a separate country and **acknowledged** its right to sign treaties, or legally binding agreements, with other countries. In treaty after treaty, the Cherokees gave more and more of their land to the United States government. In return, they gained the right to **evict** anyone who settled illegally on the remaining land. But settlers ignored these agreements. They continued to move onto Cherokee land in great numbers. The United States government did not even pretend to be **impartial** in the disputes that arose as a result. The appeals of the Cherokee leaders fell on deaf ears. The theft of their land continued **unabated.** By 1828, the Cherokee nation was one-tenth the size it had been a hundred years earlier.

In 1835, an **agent** of the United States government persuaded twenty Cherokees to sign one final treaty. According to its terms, the Cherokees would get five million dollars for leaving the last of their land and moving almost a thousand miles west. The Cherokee signers had no **authority** to act for the entire Cherokee Nation, but this fact was brushed aside as **irrelevant** by those in the government who wanted the land. The chief justice of the United States declared the agreement a **sham.** His opinion **infuriated** President Andrew Jackson, who replied, "The chief justice has made his decision; now let him enforce it."

Precisely two years after the signing of the agreement, on the orders of the president, two thousand heavily armed United States soldiers arrived on Cherokee land. They drove the Cherokee families from their homes. Nearly twenty thousand people were forced to **trek** more than nine hundred miles west into what is now Oklahoma. They went mostly on foot. It has been **estimated** that about four thousand Native Americans died on the journey, which became known as "the trail of tears." In a sense, though, the Cherokees had traveled an even longer and even more sorrowful trail, a journey in time that began when the unsuspecting Cherokees first greeted the Europeans as friends.

▶ **Answer each of the following questions in the form of a sentence. If a question does not contain a vocabulary word from the lesson's word list, use one in your answer. Use each word only once.**

1. Why did smallpox kill so many Cherokees in such a short time?

_____

_____

2. About how many Cherokees died of smallpox in 1745?

_____

_____

3. Did the Cherokees' repeated appeals to the United States government slow down the theft of their land?

_____

_____

4. What is the meaning of **agent** as it is used in the passage?

_____

_____

5. Why was the Cherokees' last treaty a **sham?**

_____

_____

6. Why might we think that the Cherokees were successful farmers?

_____

_____

abate
acknowledge
agent
authority
devastate
epidemic
estimate
evict
impartial
industrious
infuriate
irrelevant
precise
sham
trek

7. Were those who wanted the Cherokees' land influenced by the fact that the Cherokee signers of the 1835 treaty had acted illegally?

_____

_____

8. What is the meaning of **acknowledged** as it is used in the passage?

_____

_____

9. Why do you think that President Jackson was **infuriated** by the chief justice's opinion?

_____

_____

10. What is the meaning of **authority** as it is used in the passage?

_____

_____

11. What happened when the Cherokees tried to **evict** illegal settlers?

_____

_____

12. How should the United States government have behaved in dealing with the disputes between the Cherokees and the white settlers?

_____

_____

13. How far did the Cherokees have to travel to get to what is now Oklahoma?

_____

_____

14. Is the figure of 20,000 persons forced out of their homes an exact one?

_____

_____

15. What kind of effect did the forced removal of the Cherokees from their land have on them?

_____

_____

- An **epidemic** disease spreads rapidly and affects many people. (Polio was *epidemic* in the U.S. in the 1950s.) An *endemic* disease occurs normally in an area because of the conditions in that area. (Malaria is *endemic* to tropical Africa.)

- **Trek** comes from an old Dutch word *treck,* meaning "to pull or drag." Dutch settlers in South Africa used the word when describing their journeys by covered wagon because they often had to drag the wagons themselves. The English word, therefore, has come to mean any long, slow, difficult journey.

- *Industry* is a noun and means (1) "a branch of business or manufacturing" (the automobile *industry;* the film *industry*), and (2) "a willingness to work hard" (The teacher praised the student's *industry*). The two adjectives formed from this noun relate to its two different meanings. *Industrial* means "having to do with business or manufacturing." (The United States and Japan are two of the world's leading *industrial* nations.) **Industrious** relates to the second meaning of *industry*.

abate
acknowledge
agent
authority
devastate
epidemic
estimate
evict
impartial
industrious
infuriate
irrelevant
precise
sham
trek

Lesson **2**

For more practice and games, go to **www.WordlyWise3000.com**.

| **Word List** | Study the definitions of the words. Then do the exercises that follow. |

astute
ə stoot´

adj. Wise in a clever or practical way.
An **astute** shopper compares prices carefully before making a purchase.

authentic
ô then´ tik

adj. Genuine; true.
An authority on old maps declared that the sixteenth-century chart of the Florida keys is **authentic.**

authenticity *n.* (ô then tis´ i tē) The condition of being genuine.
Lawyers questioned the **authenticity** of the signature on the agreement.

authenticate *v.* To prove that something is genuine.
Only an art expert can **authenticate** the painting as one by Rubens.

delicacy
del´ i kə sē

n. 1. A choice item of food.
Smoked salmon is a **delicacy.**

2. Great consideration for the feelings of others.
Discussing her mistake will embarrass her unless you handle the matter with **delicacy.**

derogatory
də räg´ ə tôr ē

adj. Expressing a low opinion; intended to hurt the reputation of a person or thing.
His habit of making **derogatory** comments about his co-workers made him unpopular.

devour
də vour´

v. 1. To eat up hungrily.
The wolf was about to **devour** Little Red Riding Hood when the woodcutter arrived.

2. To take in eagerly with the eyes or ears.
The children **devoured** comic books when they were younger.

figment
fig´ mənt

n. Something that is made up in the mind but that has no connection with reality.
The monster in the closet is a **figment** of the child's imagination.

mythical
mith´ i kəl

adj. Imaginary; not real.
Unicorns are **mythical** creatures.

plumage
ploom´ ij

n. A bird's feathers.
Parrots have brightly colored **plumage.**

predatory
pred´ ə tôr ē

adj. 1. Living by killing and eating other animals.
Crocodiles are **predatory** reptiles.

2. Living by robbing or stealing from others.
Predatory bands of pirates once sailed the Mediterranean seeking victims.

predator *n.* 1. A creature that lives by killing.
A sea eagle is a **predator** that dives for fish.

2. A person who lives by robbing.
These gang members are **predators** who belong in jail.

prior
prī´ ər

adj. 1. Coming earlier in time.
I was unable to see you this morning because I had a **prior** appointment.

2. Coming before in order or importance.
The court ruled that the Native Americans had a **prior** claim to the land.

scavenge
skav´ ənj

v. To search through or pick over, looking for something usable.
People with metal detectors **scavenge** the beach looking for coins.

scavenger *n.* 1. Someone who scavenges.
After the fire, **scavengers** looked through the debris, hoping to find something of value.

2. An animal that feeds on dead or decaying matter.
Vultures, hyenas, and other **scavengers** are an important part of nature's clean-up crew.

slaughter
slôt´ ər

v. 1. To kill in order to obtain meat.
The hogs are fattened up before they are **slaughtered.**

2. To kill people or animals in large numbers or in a cruel way.
For centuries, whales were **slaughtered** for their oil and other valuable products.

n. 1. The killing of an animal for food.
The **slaughter** of beef cattle should be carried out as swiftly and painlessly as possible.

2. The act of killing on a large scale or in a cruel way.
Those who drink and drive contribute to the **slaughter** on the nation's highways.

solitude
säl´ ə tōod

n. The condition of being alone or at some distance from people.
We enjoyed the **solitude** of a walk on the deserted beach.

ungainly
un gān´ lē

adj. Moving in a clumsy or awkward way.
Walruses, graceful in the water, are **ungainly** creatures on land.

vulnerable
vul´ nər ə bəl

adj. Open to attack; easily injured physically or emotionally.
Starving people are more **vulnerable** to disease than those who are well fed.

Choose two phrases to form a sentence that correctly uses a word from Word List 2. Write each sentence in the space provided.

1. (a) To authenticate is to   (c) prove to be a fake.
   (b) To scavenge is to   (d) search for something usable.
   _____b____d_____

   _____

2. (a) Plumage is   (c) Delicacy is
   (b) being cut off from society.   (d) a bird's feathers.
   _____a____d_____

   _____

3. (a) that isn't real.   (c) A mythical creature is one
   (b) An astute creature is one   (d) that moves awkwardly.
   _____c_____a_____

   _____

4. (a) A figment is   (c) a choice item of food.
   (b) A delicacy is   (d) an awkward situation.
   _____b____d_____

   _____

5. (a) Authenticity is   (c) the fear of looking foolish.
   (b) Solitude is   (d) the quality of being genuine.
   _____a____d_____

   _____

6. (a) A predator is   (c) something that is imagined.
   (b) a creature that is easily hurt.   (d) A figment is
   _____d____c_____

   _____

7. (a) A prior commitment   (c) is one made in a hurry.
   (b) is one made earlier.   (d) An astute commitment
   _____a____b_____

   _____

8. (a) An ungainly person   (c) is one who takes from others.
   (b) A vulnerable person   (d) is one who is easily hurt.
   _____b____d_____

   _____

9. (a) Slaughter is   (c) killing on a large scale.
   (b) Solitude is   (d) the condition of being overcrowded.

   _____a____c_____

   _____

10. (a) An ungainly person is   (c) one who robs others.
    (b) one who is surefooted.   (d) A predatory person is

    _____d____c_____

    _____

2B ▶ Just the Right Word

Improve each of the following sentences by crossing out the bold phrase and replacing it with a word (or a form of the word) from Word List 2.

1. *astute*
   People who are **able to use good judgment** are unlikely to be fooled easily.

2. *slaughter*
   The **killing on a huge scale** of the American bison almost led to its extinction.

3. *devour*
   While at camp, Carlotta **read with great eagerness** the letters from home.

4. *scavengers*
   Persons who pick over objects that have been thrown away are not allowed at the town dump.

5. *authentic*
   It's obvious that this coin marked 55 B.C.E. is not **genuine** but must be a fake.

6. *prior*
   There is some unfinished business left over from a **meeting that took place before the present** meeting.

7. *ungainly*
   I felt very **clumsy and not at all graceful** when asked to dance in public.

8. *solitude*
   People who like **the condition of being all alone** make good lighthouse keepers.

9. *derogatory*
   I try to ignore statements that are **intended to hurt someone's reputation.**

10. The counselor asked questions about the student's family with **much consideration for his feelings.** *delicacy*

Word List

astute
authentic
delicacy
derogatory
devour
figment
mythical
plumage
predatory
prior
scavenge
slaughter
solitude
ungainly
vulnerable

Circle the letter or letters of each correct answer. A question may have more than one correct answer.

1. Which of the following might be **vulnerable?**
   (a) a young child
   (b) a wounded animal
   (c) an undefended city
   (d) a trusting person

2. In which of the following places might you find **solitude?**
   (a) a busy airport
   (b) a crowded theater
   (c) a log cabin in Alaska
   (d) an uninhabited island

3. Which of the following can be **astute?**
   (a) a reply
   (b) a person
   (c) a solution
   (d) an advertisement

4. Which of the following occurred **prior** to 1990?
   (a) the 2000 Olympics
   (b) the 2004 World Series
   (c) the 1984 Olympics
   (d) the 1993 Florida hurricane

5. Which of the following are **mythical** creatures?
   (a) mermaids
   (b) unicorns
   (c) dragons
   (d) dinosaurs

6. Which of the following are **predators?**
   (a) wolves
   (b) gorillas
   (c) spiders
   (d) sharks

7. Which of the following might be **devoured?**
   (a) important news
   (b) an interesting novel
   (c) a batch of cookies
   (d) elevator music

8. Which of the following is a **derogatory** remark?
   (a) "You're stupid."
   (b) "It's too expensive."
   (c) "You're a saint."
   (d) "You could do better."

Each group of four words contains either two synonyms or two antonyms. Circle that pair. Then circle the S if they are synonyms or the A if they are antonyms.

1. derogatory	ungainly	authentic	fake		S	A
2. impartial	mythical	prior	real		S	A
3. astute	ungainly	stupid	precise		S	A
4. figment	slaughter	killing	solitude		S	A
5. irrelevant	earlier	prior	derogatory		S	A

Complete the analogies by selecting the pair of words whose relationship most resembles the relationship of the pair in capital letters. Circle the letter of the pair you choose.

6. NIBBLE : DEVOUR ::
   - (a) abate : increase
   - (b) lose : scavenge
   - (c) guess : estimate
   - (d) annoy : infuriate

7. PREDATOR : PREDATORY ::
   - (a) author : authentic
   - (b) victim : vulnerable
   - (c) precision : precise
   - (d) solitude : alone

8. DELICACY : EAT ::
   - (a) jewelry : decorate
   - (b) beverage : drink
   - (c) food : delicious
   - (d) nose : cold

9. PLUMAGE : BIRD ::
   - (a) wheels : car
   - (b) feather : wings
   - (c) water : boat
   - (d) scales : reptile

10. GRACEFUL : UNGAINLY ::
    - (a) slow : slower
    - (b) flattering : derogatory
    - (c) mythical : imaginary
    - (d) prior : earlier

astute
authentic
delicacy
derogatory
devour
figment
mythical
plumage
predatory
prior
scavenge
slaughter
solitude
ungainly
vulnerable

Read the passage. Then answer the questions that follow it.

The Last Dodo

If someone called you a "dodo," you would probably be insulted. It is a **derogatory** term that describes someone who is not very **astute.** The English word comes from the Portuguese *doudo,* which means "a foolish person." Dodo was the name Portuguese settlers gave to a large bird that inhabited the island of Mauritius in the Indian Ocean. Some people think of the dodo as a **mythical** creature. It was a real bird, however, and its story is a sad one.

For thousands of years, until the island of Mauritius was discovered by Portuguese sailors in 1507, this odd-looking bird lived in peaceful **solitude.** Because there were no **predatory** animals on the island, the dodo had long since lost the ability to fly. And since it had no natural enemies, it was very trusting and made no attempt to flee when approached by humans. Because of this, the Portuguese considered the bird stupid. They gave it the name by which we know it today—the dodo.

Even if it had been less trusting of humans, the dodo would still have been **vulnerable.** It was too fat and **ungainly** to run very fast. The settlers on the island found that dodos, although a little tough, were good to eat. They **slaughtered** them in large numbers. Domesticated animals brought to the island by the settlers added to the dodos' problems. The female dodo laid a single large white egg, which it deposited on the ground, usually in a tuft of grass. **Prior** to the arrival of the first settlers, the eggs had lain undisturbed until they hatched. To the dogs that now roamed the island, these eggs were a **delicacy;** the dogs **scavenged** the island and **devoured** any dodo eggs they found. The dodo was last seen alive in 1681. None is believed to have survived after that date.

As time passed, people began to wonder if the dodo had ever existed. Drawings done by artists who had visited Mauritius showed a bird somewhat larger than a swan, with a long neck, a large head, an enormous black bill, and a short, tufty tail. Its **plumage** was grayish in color over most of its body and white on its breast. Most people who saw these pictures thought that such an odd-looking creature must be a **figment** of the artist's imagination; at that time, there was no way of knowing whether they provided an **authentic** record of an actual creature.

Then, in 1889, a large number of dodo bones were discovered in a swamp on Mauritius. Several skeletons were reconstructed from them and later displayed in museums in London and Paris. They are all that remain of this odd-looking but rather lovable bird.

▶ **Answer each of the following questions in the form of a sentence. If a question does not contain a vocabulary word from the lesson's word list, use one in your answer. Use each word only once.**

1. What drastic change occurred in the dodos' living conditions in 1507?

_____

_____

2. What is the meaning of **prior** as it is used in the passage?

_____

_____

3. What was it about the dodo's nature that made it easy to catch?

_____

_____

4. What was it about the dodo's physical condition that made it easy to catch?

_____

_____

5. What other names of birds are **derogatory** when applied to humans?

_____

_____

6. How was the existence of the dodo **authenticated?**

_____

_____

7. What did the Portuguese think of the dodo's intelligence?

_____

_____

8. What is the meaning of **delicacy** as it is used in the passage?

_____

_____

astute
authentic
delicacy
derogatory
devour
figment
mythical
plumage
predatory
prior
scavenge
slaughter
solitude
ungainly
vulnerable

9. What color were the feathers of a dodo?

_____

_____

10. What is the meaning of **devoured** as it is used in the passage?

_____

_____

11. Why did many people believe the dodo to be a **figment** of an artist's imagination?

_____

_____

12. What did many people come to think about the dodo before the discovery of the bones?

_____

_____

13. What is the meaning of **slaughtered** as it is used in the passage?

_____

_____

14. What is the meaning of **predatory** as it is used in the passage?

_____

_____

15. How would you describe the dogs that lived on the island?

_____

_____

- The Latin for *feather* is *pluma*. In addition to the word **plumage,** this Latin root gives us the English word *plume,* which is a noun, meaning "a large feather or group of feathers," and a verb, meaning "to smooth its feathers." (Birds *plume* themselves with their beaks.) The French word for *pen* is *plume* and comes from the same Latin root. Pens were once made from large feathers with the ends split to hold ink.

- The Latin *solus* means "alone" or "without company" and forms the root of a number of English words in addition to **solitude.** *Solitaire* is a card game for just one person. *Solitary* means "alone" or "without company." *Solo* means "performed by one person."

astute

authentic

delicacy

derogatory

devour

figment

mythical

plumage

predatory

prior

scavenge

slaughter

solitude

ungainly

vulnerable

For more practice and games, go to www.WordlyWise3000.com.

Word List

Study the definitions of the words. Then do the exercises that follow.

admonish
ad män´ ish

v. 1. To warn.
Rescue workers **admonished** us to stay away from the flooding river.

2. To criticize gently.
The coach **admonished** me for missing practice.

admonition *n.* (ad mə nish´ ən) A warning.
We remembered our parents' **admonition** to stay close to shore while swimming.

aghast
ə gast´

adj. Struck with horror; shocked.
We were **aghast** at the photographs of starving children in Africa.

annihilate
ə nī´ ə lāt

v. To destroy completely; to reduce to utter ruin.
General Custer's army of over 200 men was **annihilated** at the battle of the Little Bighorn in 1876.

benefactor
ben´ ə fak tər

n. A person who provides help, especially by giving money.
People who donated more than $100 were listed as **benefactors** of the library.

bestow
bē stō´

v. To give as an honor; to present as a gift.
An Academy Award is the highest honor Hollywood can **bestow** on a film.

devious
dē´ vē əs

adj. 1. Having many twists and turns; winding.
The climbers followed a **devious** route up the mountain.

2. Sneaky; not frank or honest.
This **devious** scheme was intended to take advantage of vulnerable people.

devoid
də void´

adj. Lacking; empty; entirely without.
Although he had experienced great misfortune, he was **devoid** of bitterness.

heed
hēd

v. To pay attention to.
I hope you will **heed** my advice.

n. Attention; notice.
Pay **heed** to the teacher's instructions before you begin the test.

heedful *adj.* Paying careful attention.
Heedful of the fog, I drove slowly.

heedless *adj.* Failing to pay proper attention.
They went ahead with their plans, **heedless** of our objections.

mortal môrt´l	*n.* A human being, especially as contrasted with a god. Achilles, a hero in Greek mythology, had a goddess for a mother and a **mortal** for a father. *adj.* 1. Of or relating to human beings. Being **mortal,** he accepted the fact that one day he would die. 2. Causing death; fatal. India's Prime Minister Indira Gandhi received a **mortal** wound delivered by an assassin in 1984. 3. Very severe. My friend wouldn't go into the reptile house because he has a **mortal** fear of snakes.
muse myo͞oz	*v.* To think about in a quiet, careful way. I **mused** over whether to sell the house.
pioneer pī ə nir´	*n.* A person who goes before others and opens the way for them to follow. Lucretia Mott and Elizabeth Cady Stanton, two nineteenth-century women, were **pioneers** in the women's rights movement. *v.* To open the way for others. Isadora Duncan **pioneered** modern dance.
plague plāg	*n.* 1. A deadly disease that spreads rapidly from person to person. Those Londoners who could afford it fled to the country to escape the great **plague** of 1665. 2. Anything that causes destruction or suffering. A **plague** of locusts destroyed the crop. *v.* To cause suffering or distress. After the tryouts, I was **plagued** by doubts that I would make the varsity team.
subside səb sīd´	*v.* 1. To sink to a lower level. After the rain stopped, the floodwaters gradually **subsided.** 2. To become quieter or less active. The baby's sobs gradually **subsided.**
unwitting un wit´iŋ	*adj.* Not done on purpose; unintended. I tried to ignore the **unwitting** insult, but his comment hurt me just the same.
wrath rath	*n.* Forceful anger; fury. It says in the Bible that envy and **wrath** shorten life. **wrathful** *adj.* Very angry. In Homer's story of the Trojan War, a **wrathful** Achilles seeks revenge on the killer of his friend Patroclus.

Choose two phrases to form a sentence that correctly uses a word from Word List 3. Write each sentence in the space provided.

1. (a) is one that is caused deliberately.   (c) is one that causes death.
   (b) A mortal wound   (d) An unwitting injury

   _____B , C_____

2. (a) helps with gifts of money.   (c) stands in the way of change.
   (b) A pioneer is someone who   (d) A benefactor is someone who

   _____D , A_____

3. (a) one that is unintended.   (c) one given as a warning.
   (b) A wrathful insult is   (d) An unwitting insult is

   _____D , A_____

4. (a) gradually rises.   (c) A subsiding path is one that
   (b) twists and turns.   (d) A devious path is one that

   _____D , B_____

5. (a) fooled by false promises.   (c) To be aghast is to be
   (b) shocked.   (d) To be annihilated is to be

   _____C , B_____

6. (a) To subside is to   (c) To muse is to
   (b) do worse than expected.   (d) sink to a lower level.

   _____A , D_____

7. (a) To be wrathful is to   (c) live forever.
   (b) To be mortal is to   (d) be very angry.

   _____A , D_____

8. (a) open the way for others.   (c) To muse is to
   (b) express disagreement.   (d) To pioneer is to

   _____D , A_____

9. (a) To admonish someone is to (c) To plague someone is to
   (b) protect that person. (d) criticize that person.

   A, B

10. (a) is to fail to pay attention to it. (c) To be heedless of something
    (b) is to be well supplied with it. (d) To be devoid of something

    C, A

3B ▶ Just the Right Word

Improve each of the following sentences by crossing out the bold phrase and replacing it with a word (or a form of the word) from Word List 3.

1. "Lord, what fools these **human beings** be," says Shakespeare's Puck. *mortals*

2. Drug-related violence is a **cause of much suffering** that began to spread rapidly in the 1970s. *plague*

3. Homestead Air Force Base in Florida was almost **reduced to ruins** in 1992 by Hurricane Andrew. *anniahtated*

4. Elizabeth Blackwell was a **person who opened the way for others** in the field of medical education for women. *pionere*

5. Smokers should **pay close attention to** the warnings on cigarette packages. *heed*

6. Avoid doing business with Ed; he is **not honest in his dealings with others.** *devious*

7. As far as we know, Mars is **totally lacking in any form** of life. *devoid*

8. In ancient times, people believed that a volcano's eruption was caused by the **terrible anger** of the gods. *wrath*

9. Two children are easier to care for than one, he **thought quietly to himself.** *muese*

10. We obeyed the park ranger's **instruction that warned us** to be careful with matches while in the woods. *admonished*

admonish
aghast
annihilate
benefactor
bestow
devious
devoid
heed
mortal
muse
pioneer
plague
subside
unwitting
wrath

Circle the letter or letters of each correct answer. A question may have more than one correct answer.

1. Which of the following can **subside?**
   (a) an epidemic
   (b) the floor
   (c) a storm
   (d) flame

2. Which of the following might a **wrathful** person do?
   (a) seek revenge
   (b) apologize
   (c) make derogatory remarks
   (d) speak in a loud voice

3. Which of the following can you **heed?**
   (a) advice
   (b) a suggestion
   (c) a warning
   (d) a gift

4. Which of the following might **plague** a person?
   (a) hopes
   (b) doubts
   (c) worries
   (d) fears

5. Which of the following might make you **aghast?**
   (a) seeing a beautiful sunset
   (b) hearing of a terrible accident
   (c) missing a favorite TV show
   (d) receiving good news

6. Which of the following can be **mortal?**
   (a) terror
   (b) wounds
   (c) buildings
   (d) horses

7. Which of the following could be described as **devious?**
   (a) a winding path
   (b) an impartial judge
   (c) a person who lies and cheats
   (d) a person who lacks authority

8. Which of the following might a **benefactor** do?
   (a) pay your college tuition
   (b) support a local theater
   (c) make derogatory remarks about you
   (d) give you good advice

Many English words come from Latin. We say they have Latin roots.

Read these Latin words and their meanings. Then fill in the blank spaces in the sentences. The vocabulary words are from this or earlier lessons.

facere (to make)	*furor* (rage)	*monere* (to warn)	*mors* (death)
nihil (nothing)	*sidere* (to settle)	*solus* (alone)	*pars* (side)
via (way)	*vulnus* (a wound)		

1. To _admonish_ someone is to warn that person. The word comes from the Latin _monere_ , meaning _to warn_ .

2. _solotude_ is the state of being alone. The word comes from the Latin _solus_ , meaning _alone_ .

3. To be _vonerable_ is to be easily hurt. The word comes from the Latin _____ , meaning _____ .

4. To _anihalate_ something is to destroy it completely. The word comes from the Latin _____ , meaning _____ .

5. An _impatal_ judge will hear both sides of an argument fairly. The word comes from the Latin _____ , meaning _____ .

6. To _infuroate_ someone is to make him extremely angry. The word comes from the Latin _furor_ , meaning _rage_ .

7. A _devioue_ person is one who is not direct and straightforward. The word comes from the Latin _____ , meaning _____ .

8. To _subside_ is to fall to a lower level. The word comes from the Latin _____ , meaning _____ .

9. A _mortal_ wound is one that causes death. The word comes from the Latin _____ , meaning _____ .

10. A _____ is a person who tries to make things better for others. The word comes from the Latin _____ , meaning _____ .

admonish
aghast
annihilate
benefactor
bestow
devious
devoid
heed
mortal
muse
pioneer
plague
subside
unwitting
wrath

Read the passage. Then answer the questions that follow it.

Pandora's Box

Modern English contains many words and phrases whose origins go back to ancient Greece. One of these phrases is a *Pandora's Box,* which has come to mean "something that produces unexpected problems or difficulties." Take, for example, the nineteenth-century French scientist Marie Curie. She was a **pioneer** in the study of uranium, and it could be said that she opened a Pandora's Box with her research. Her work led to the splitting of the uranium atom and the development of the atomic bomb. This gave the human race, for the first time in history, the power to **annihilate** itself. The expression a Pandora's Box comes from a Greek myth that explains how evil and suffering came into existence in a world that was originally **devoid** of them.

The story starts with Prometheus, whom the ancient Greeks looked upon as a **benefactor** of the human race. They believed that he stole fire from Zeus, the king of the gods, and gave it to human beings. To get revenge, the **wrathful** Zeus punished Prometheus by chaining him to a rock where eagles came and devoured his liver. Each night it grew back, and each day it was devoured afresh. Zeus was not satisfied with this, however; he also wanted to punish the people who had received the precious gift of fire, so he came up with a **devious** plan.

Zeus ordered his son Hephaestus, the best craftsman of the gods, to create the first woman. Her name, Pandora, means "all the gifts" because each of the gods **bestowed** a special gift upon her. Aphrodite gave her beauty. Hermes gave her the ability to be crafty. Zeus gave her a box, which he **admonished** her never to open. But he also gave her the gift of curiosity. He knew that she would not **heed** his warning.

Zeus then sent Pandora to live on Earth as a **mortal.** She married and lived happily, untroubled except for one thing. She could not stop glancing at the box that Zeus had given her. That kept her **musing** about what it contained. She was often tempted to lift the lid and peep inside. Then she would remember Zeus's warning and restrain herself. However, her curiosity, far from **subsiding,** increased with every passing day.

Finally, Pandora could stand it no longer. She acted swiftly, so as to give herself no time to think. She picked up the box and opened it. Immediately, all the evils that now exist in the world flew out of Pandora's Box. Greed and envy, hatred and fear, disease and despair; all appeared on Earth for the first time. They began to **plague** humankind. Pandora was **aghast** at what she had done. She quickly slammed the lid shut. Too late! She had been Zeus's **unwitting** helper as he carried out his plan of revenge and proved his power once again.

▶ **Answer each of the following questions in the form of a sentence. If a question does not contain a vocabulary word from the lesson's word list, use one in your answer. Use each word only once.**

1. What did Prometheus **bestow** on humankind?

   Five

2. What is the meaning of **subsiding** as it is used in the passage?

   lowering

3. Did Pandora know what she was doing when she helped Zeus carry out his plan?

   no

4. Why would it be incorrect to call Pandora a **benefactor** of humankind?

   yes

5. What is the meaning of **devious** as it is used in the passage?

   cunning

6. What warning did Zeus give Pandora when he presented her with the box?

   not to open it

7. Did Hephaestus obey Zeus's order?

   no

admonish

aghast

annihilate

benefactor

bestow

devious

devoid

heed

mortal

muse

pioneer

plague

subside

unwitting

wrath

8. How did Zeus's gift of curiosity affect Pandora?

She opend it

9. What is the meaning of **plague** as it is used in the passage?

bad

10. Did Zeus show any pity for Prometheus?

_no_

11. In what way did Marie Curie take a lead in the world of science?

Radiation

12. What is the meaning of **mortal** as it is used in the passage?

a peson

13. According to the myth, who suffered because of Zeus's **wrath?**

people

14. Why can we say that Marie Curie opened a Pandora's Box?

Radiation

15. How do you think Madame Curie would have felt if she had known that her research would lead to the atom bomb?

happy

- The word **benefactor** is formed from two Latin roots, *bene,* which means "good" or "well," and *facare,* which means "to do; to make." The Latin word *malus* means "bad" or "evil." Using your knowledge of Latin roots, can you figure out the meaning of the word *malefactor?*

- The Latin word for "death" is *mortalis;* from it comes our word **mortal.** The antonym of *mortal,* both as an adjective and a noun, is *immortal.* As an adjective, it means "living forever" (According to Greek mythology, the gods and goddesses who lived on Mount Olympus were *immortal*), and "having lasting fame" (No writer can compare to the *immortal* William Shakespeare). As a noun, *immortal* means "a mythical being who will never die" (Athena and the other *immortals* of Mount Olympus were sometimes rivals), and "a person having lasting fame" (Jane Austen is one of the *immortals* of English literature).

- **Plague** is now the general term for any widespread and deadly disease; it once referred to a specific disease called "the Plague," also known as "the Black Death," which swept through Europe and parts of Asia in the fourteenth century, killing up to three quarters of the population. A red cross on a door was a sign that someone inside the house had the disease. Spread by fleas that had bitten infected rats, it attacked many parts of the body, especially the lungs, and was almost always fatal. It has reappeared at various times over recorded history; the last great outbreak of the disease was in England in 1665.

admonish

aghast

annihilate

benefactor

bestow

devious

devoid

heed

mortal

muse

pioneer

plague

subside

unwitting

wrath

For more practice and games, go to **www.WordlyWise3000.com**.

Word List

Study the definitions of the words. Then do the exercises that follow.

acquire
ə kwīr´

v. To gain ownership of something; to get by one's own efforts or actions.
Most tourists **acquire** souvenirs from the places they visit.

acquisition *n.* (ak wə zish´ ən) Something that is acquired.
We left the store with our shopping bags filled with our **acquisitions.**

antagonize
an tag´ ə nīz

v. To make an enemy of; to stir up anger or dislike.
You will **antagonize** your classmates if you make derogatory comments about them.

competent
käm´ pə tənt

adj. Having the ability to do what is needed.
The mechanic is **competent** to work on the car's brakes.

competence *n.* The ability to do what is needed.
This examination tests the student's **competence** to drive safely.

comprise
kəm prīz´

v. 1. To form; to make up.
Six states **comprise** New England.

2. To consist of or include.
A baseball team **comprises** nine players.

correspond
kôr ə spänd´

v. 1. To match; to be equal to.
The two handwriting samples **correspond** in every way.

2. To exchange letters with another person.
Although the friends hadn't seen each other for several years, they **corresponded** regularly.

correspondence *n.* The act of exchanging letters; the letters that are exchanged.
The **correspondence** of famous people is often published after their death.

dilapidated
di lap´ ə dāt əd

adj. In poor condition from neglect or age.
The shed was so **dilapidated** that it wasn't worth repairing.

illustrious
il lus´ trē əs

adj. Very famous; outstanding.
V. S. Naipaul, the **illustrious** West Indian writer, received the Nobel Prize for Literature in 2001.

incident
in´ sə dənt

n. Something that happens in real life or in a story; an event, often of little importance.
My car was struck from behind, but I thought no more about the **incident** until my neck began to hurt.

inherit
in her´ it

v. 1. To receive something from someone after that person's death.
I **inherited** this house from my grandparents.

2. To receive, as part of one's physical or mental make-up, from one's parents.
The baby **inherited** his mother's red hair.

---

latitude
lat´ ə tōōd

n. 1. The distance north or south of the equator, measured in degrees.
The **latitude** of New Orleans is 30 degrees north.

2. A region as marked by its distance from the equator.
Tropical plants cannot survive in northern **latitudes.**

3. Freedom from strict rules.
Students in high school are allowed some **latitude** in choosing their courses.

---

loath
lōth

adj. Unwilling; reluctant.
I was **loath** to put my trust in such a devious person.

---

maintain
mān tān´

v. 1. To declare something to be true.
Although the evidence against her is strong, she continues to **maintain** her innocence.

2. To continue in the same way or condition.
The walkers try to **maintain** an even pace as they exercise.

3. To keep in good condition.
The state of New York **maintains** this highway.

---

renovate
ren´ ə vāt

v. To make like new again.
We intend to **renovate** the apartment completely before we move in.

renovation *n.* (ren ə vā´ shən) The act of renovating; the thing renovated.
A group of concerned parents was responsible for the **renovation** of the playground.

---

reprimand
rep´ rə mand

v. To scold in a harsh or formal manner.
The manager **reprimanded** us for being late for work.

n. A strong scolding from someone in authority.
The teacher gave us a **reprimand** for being absent without permission.

---

supervise
sōō´ pər vīz

v. To direct or manage activities.
Ms. Agostino will **supervise** the students in the study hall.

supervision *n.* (sōō´ pər vizh´ ən) The act of managing or directing.
A lack of proper **supervision** resulted in yesterday's accident at the playground.

supervisor *n.* A person who manages or directs activities.
The **supervisor** reminded the worker to wear a hardhat at the construction site.

Choose two phrases to form a sentence that correctly uses a word from Word List 4. Write each sentence in the space provided.

1. (a) something caused by carelessness.
   (b) An incident is
   (c) A renovation is
   (d) something made like new again.

   _C, D_ _____

   _____

2. (a) To supervise someone is to
   (b) To antagonize someone is to
   (c) make that person angry.
   (d) pay no heed to that person.

   _B, C_ _____

   _____

3. (a) receive it after another person's death.
   (b) allow it to fall into neglect.
   (c) To maintain property is to
   (d) To inherit property is to

   _D, A_ _____

   _____

4. (a) keep them in good condition.
   (b) consist of them.
   (c) To comprise several buildings is to
   (d) To acquire several buildings is to

   _C, B_ _____

   _____

5. (a) distance from the equator.
   (b) letters exchanged between people.
   (c) Latitude is
   (d) Competence is

   _C, A_ _____

   _____

6. (a) To be illustrious is to be
   (b) heavily decorated.
   (c) To be dilapidated is to be
   (d) in a poor state of repair.

   _C, D_ _____

   _____

7. (a) something that takes place.
   (b) an unwitting insult or injury.
   (c) A reprimand is
   (d) An incident is

   _D, A_ _____

   _____

8. (a) Correspondence is   (c) failure to do what is required.
   (b) letters exchanged   (d) Competence is
      between people.

   _____A, B_____

9. (a) a severe scolding.   (c) A supervisor is
   (b) a speech of praise.   (d) A reprimand is

   _____D, A_____

10. (a) To acquire a positive attitude   (c) is to question its value.
    (b) To maintain a positive attitude   (d) is to continue to have it.

    _____B, D_____

4B ▶ Just the Right Word

Improve each of the following sentences by crossing out the bold phrase and replacing it with a word (or a form of the word) from Word List 4.

1. I was told that I would **on the death of my mother become the new owner of** the property. 9

2. In what year did the museum **become the owner of** this painting? |

3. I was having such a good time that I was **not quite willing** to leave. ||

4. Joe is too young to play outside without **someone watching over him.** 15

5. A pen and paper **form or make up** this writer's basic equipment. 12

6. We feel it is important to **write letters to each other** now that we live so far apart. 5

7. The owner never doubted the manager's **ability to do the job properly.** 3

8. Maya Angelou is one of America's most **brilliant and highly respected** poets. 7

1 acquire
2 antagonize
3 competent
4 comprise
5 correspond
6 dilapidated
7 illustrious
8 incident
9 inherit
10 latitude
11 loath
12 maintain
13 renovate
14 reprimand
15 supervise

14

9. Students in that school are given plenty of **freedom from strict rules** but are expected to act responsibly.

12

10. A crew of sixty workers is needed to **take proper care of** the town's parks during the summer.

4C Applying Meanings

Circle the letter or letters of each correct answer. A question may have more than one correct answer.

1. Which of the following might be **inherited?**
   (a) brown eyes
   (b) bad luck
   (c) money
   (d) time

2. Which of the following can be **maintained?**
   (a) a point of view
   (b) a friendship
   (c) a building
   (d) a custom

3. Which of the following might be **supervised?**
   (a) a work crew
   (b) a play group
   (c) the building of a house
   (d) solitude

4. Which of the following might result in a **reprimand?**
   (a) behaving selfishly
   (b) telling a lie
   (c) getting sick
   (d) getting an "A" on a test

5. Which of the following could be **renovated?**
   (a) a house
   (b) a tree
   (c) a pet
   (d) a disease

6. Which of the following could be an **acquisition?**
   (a) intelligence
   (b) old age
   (c) a painting
   (d) a quarrel

7. The word **latitude** could be applied to which of the following?
   (a) 45 degrees south
   (b) 10 degrees east
   (c) North America
   (d) the North Star

8. Which of the following could be **dilapidated?**
   (a) a building   (c) a haircut
   (b) a truck   (d) an injury

A suffix is a word part that comes at the end of a word. One of the things a suffix can do is change a word from one part of speech to another.

Change each of the verbs into a noun by changing or adding a suffix: -ence, -er, -ion, -tion, or -ment. Write the new word on the line. All words are from this or earlier lessons.

Verb	Noun
1. correspond	_____
2. renovate	_____
3. admonish	_____
4. scavenge	_____
5. acquire	_____

acquire
antagonize
competent
comprise
correspond
dilapidated
illustrious
incident
inherit
latitude
loath
maintain
renovate
reprimand
supervise

Now change the adjectives into nouns by changing, adding, or removing a suffix. Write the new word on the line. All words are from this or earlier lessons.

Adjective	Noun
6. precise	_____
7. wrathful	_____
8. competent	_____
9. devastating	_____
10. authentic	_____

Read the passage. Then answer the questions that follow it.

Mount Vernon

No visit to Washington, D.C., is complete without a trip to Mount Vernon, the home of George Washington, our nation's **illustrious** first president. It is located just a few miles south of our nation's capital. Its fine views, spacious lawns, shaded walks, and carefully tended gardens make it one of the most popular tourist attractions in the nation. More than a million people a year visit Mount Vernon. There they may pay their respects to the memory of our first president and his wife, the first lady; both are buried there.

Mount Vernon had been in the Washington family for almost a hundred years when George Washington **inherited** the property in 1761. It **comprised** five separate farms as well as the house overlooking the Potomac River in which he lived with his wife and her two children from a former marriage. Because the house was too small for their needs, Washington added rooms and outbuildings. He hired the best workers he could find and **supervised** their work closely; by the time he had finished, Mount Vernon was the fine mansion visitors see today.

Washington was **loath** to leave his beautiful home. But his duty to his country required him to be absent from Mount Vernon from 1775 until 1783. During that time he led the Continental army in the war against the British. In his absence, a distant cousin, Lund Washington, managed the property for him. We know a great deal about this period in the history of Mount Vernon because the **correspondence** between the two men has survived.

Washington gave his cousin considerable **latitude** in looking after the estate, and Lund was a **competent** manager. However, one **incident** aroused Washington's wrath. Lund wrote to him saying that a British warship had come up the river and that the crew had asked for food. Lund had not wanted to **antagonize** them. He had complied with their request. Washington **reprimanded** his cousin, telling him that he should have refused "even if they had burnt my house and laid the Plantation in ruins."

In 1789, Washington reluctantly left Mount Vernon once again to serve as the country's first president. After eight years he retired from public life and returned for the last time to his beloved home. Two years later he died. The property remained in the Washington family until 1858. By then the house was in a sadly **dilapidated** state. In that year, the Mount Vernon

Ladies Association, a group of private citizens, **acquired** the property. The association carefully **renovated** the house. It now looks as it did when George Washington lived there. The Mount Vernon Ladies Association has **maintained** it ever since and opens it to the public every day of the year.

▶ **Answer each of the following questions in the form of a sentence. If a question does not contain a vocabulary word from the lesson's word list, use one in your answer. Use each word only once.**

1. What is the meaning of **latitude** as it is used in the passage?

leeway

2. Who **supervised** the workers at Mount Vernon between 1775 and 1783?

Lund Washington

3. Was George Washington eager to leave Mount Vernon in 1789?

no

4. Why does Washington have a secure place in United States history?

He gave us freedom

5. Why did George Washington, on the whole, have reason to be satisfied with his cousin's management?

He was sufficent

6. Was George Washington at Mount Vernon when the British warship arrived?

No

7. Was George Washington pleased when his cousin helped the British?

no

acquire
antagonize
competent
comprise
correspond
dilapidated
illustrious
incident
inherit
latitude
loath
maintain
renovate
reprimand
supervise

8. What is the meaning of **comprised** as it is used in the passage?

contained

9. How did George Washington know what was going on at Mount Vernon while he was away?

letters

10. Why did Lund give the British what they asked for?

Didn't want to burn the stuff

11. What is the meaning of **inherited** as it is used in the passage?

Took juristiction of

12. Had the Washington family taken good care of Mount Vernon prior to its purchase by the Mount Vernon Ladies Association?

_No_

13. What was Mount Vernon in need of in 1858?

renovation

14. In what year did George Washington become the owner of Mount Vernon?

_1761_

15. What is the meaning of **maintained** as it is used in the passage?

taken place

- *Inheritance* is a noun related to the word list's first meaning of the verb **inherit.** An *inheritance* is the property received from a person after her or his death. Another noun that relates to the first meaning of *inherit* is *heir,* one who inherits property. *Heredity* is another noun related to the second meaning of *inherit. Heredity* is the passing on from parents to children of the things that make up that person, both physically and mentally.

- Lines of **latitude** are imaginary lines parallel to and north and south of the equator. Latitudes close to zero degrees are near the equator; latitudes close to 90 degrees are near the poles. Lines of *longitude* run from pole to pole and are measured east and west of Greenwich, England. (The *latitude* of Los Angeles is 34 degrees north; its *longitude* is 118 degrees west.)

- The Latin for *new* is *novus,* which forms the root of the verb **renovate.** Other words formed from this root include *novice,* "a person new to an activity" (a tennis *novice); novelty,* "something that excites interest because it is new" (a popular *novelty* in the stores this holiday season); and *innovation,* "a new way of doing something" (the latest *innovation* in the automobile industry).

acquire

antagonize

competent

comprise

correspond

dilapidated

illustrious

incident

inherit

latitude

loath

maintain

renovate

reprimand

supervise

Crossword Puzzle Solve the crossword puzzle by studying the clues and filling in the answer boxes. Clues followed by a number are definitions of words in Lessons 1 through 4. The number gives the word list in which the answer to the clue appears.

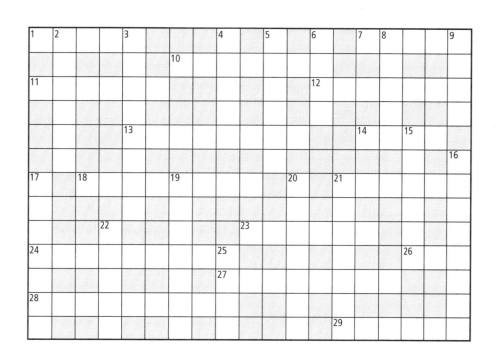

Clues Across

1. To become weaker; to decrease (1)
7. Forceful anger; fury (3)
10. Something that exists only in the mind (2)
11. Wise in a clever or practical way (2)
12. To gain ownership (4)
13. To keep in good condition (4)
14. Something fake or false (1)
18. Imaginary; not real (2)
21. A deadly disease that spreads rapidly (3)
23. To eat up hungrily (2)
24. Having the ability to do what is needed (4)
26. Comes before D E F
27. To make like new again (4)
28. To direct or manage activities (4)
29. Four score

Clues Down

2. To present as a gift (3)
3. To figure out roughly (1)
4. Something that brings about a result (1)
5. Lacking; empty (3)
6. A luminous body in the night sky
8. Opposite of *smooth*
9. To pay attention to (3)
15. Large country in central Africa
16. A choice item of food (2)
17. Exact; accurate (1)
19. To receive after the death of someone (4)
20. Not frank or honest (3)
21. Birds' feathers (2)
22. Excessive _____ on the highway can kill.
25. A long, slow, and difficult journey (1)

For more practice and games, go to **www.WordlyWise3000.com**.

Word List	Study the definitions of the words. Then do the exercises that follow.

adequate
ad´ ə kwət

adj. Enough; sufficient.
One blanket will be **adequate** on such a warm night.

administer
ad min´ is tər

v. 1. To manage or direct.
The Red Cross **administers** the blood donor program.

2. To give out as treatment or assistance.
The scout leader **administered** first aid to the child who had cut his hand.

agitate
aj´ ə tāt

v. 1. To disturb or upset.
Talk of sharks in the water **agitated** swimmers at the beach.

2. To move with an irregular, fast, or violent action.
Strong winds **agitated** the surface of the lake.

3. To stir up interest in and support for a cause.
The miners **agitated** for better working conditions.

capitulate
kə pich´ yōō lāt

v. To give in; to surrender.
The airline **capitulated** to the baggage handlers' demands and granted the pay raise.

citrus
si´ trəs

n. 1. A fruit of the family that includes oranges, lemons, grapefruits, and limes.
A **citrus** is an excellent source of vitamin C.

2. A tree that produces these fruits.
Citruses grow well in Florida.

adj. Of or relating to these fruits or trees.
The kumquat is a less well-known member of the **citrus** family.

disrupt
dis rupt´

v. 1. To break up the orderly course of.
Angry protesters **disrupted** the president's speech.

2. To interrupt; to bring to a temporary halt.
A strike by the drivers **disrupted** service on the subway.

disruptive *adj.* Causing confusion or disorder.
Disruptive behavior is not acceptable in the classroom.

disruption *n.* A disturbance that interrupts or causes confusion.
Work on the telephone lines caused a temporary **disruption** of service.

hovel
huv´ əl

n. An unpleasant, cramped, and dilapidated place to live.
The Saxons complained that they were forced to live in **hovels** while their Norman conquerers had fine homes.

illiterate il lit´ ər ət	*adj.* Unable to read or write. Volunteers are needed to help teach **illiterate** adults how to read. **illiteracy** *n.* Inability to read or write. **Illiteracy** is practically nonexistent in Japan.
indifferent in dif´ ər ənt	*adj.* 1. Not concerned about; not caring. The authorities can no longer afford to be **indifferent** to the problem of nuclear waste disposal. 2. Neither very good nor very bad; passable. Her **indifferent** grades in school worried her parents.
menial mē´ nē əl	*adj.* Of or relating to low-level, humble work. Desperate for money, Oliver accepted **menial** work with low pay.
permanent pʉr´ mə nənt	*adj.* Lasting or expected to last for a long time. A child's first **permanent** teeth appear at about the age of six.
respite res´ pit	*n.* A period of rest; a pause. The rain brought a welcome **respite** from the tremendous heat.
strenuous stren´ yo͞o əs	*adj.* 1. Needing much effort; using a lot of energy. Chopping wood is **strenuous** work. 2. Very active; vigorous. The plan to close the local school met with **strenuous** opposition from parents.
toil toil	*v.* 1. To work long and hard. Sugar cane cutters **toil** in the fields from dawn to dusk. 2. To make one's way with difficulty. We **toiled** up the steep hill. *n.* Hard and tiring labor. After a lifetime of **toil,** her retirement is a richly deserved reward.
urgent ʉr´ jənt	*adj.* Needing quick action or attention. The county has an **urgent** need for a new hospital. **urgency** *n.* The need for quick action. The senator stressed the **urgency** of cleaning up the polluted waters of our country.

Choose two phrases to form a sentence that correctly uses a word from Word List 5. Write each sentence in the space provided.

1. (a) work long and hard.　　(c) To toil is to
   (b) To capitulate is to　　(d) move with an irregular, violent action.

_____

_____

2. (a) that can be taken two ways.　　(c) that is expressed with force.
   (b) A strenuous response is one　　(d) An indifferent response is one

_____

_____

3. (a) Illiteracy is　　(c) the inability to read or write.
   (b) Urgency is　　(d) an unwillingness to be concerned.

_____

_____

4. (a) a building to house animals.　　(c) A hovel is
   (b) A respite is　　(d) a small and dilapidated house.

_____

_____

5. (a) avoid the company of others.　　(c) To be indifferent is to
   (b) be merely passable.　　(d) To be permanent is to

_____

_____

6. (a) To agitate　　(c) is to surrender.
   (b) is to become bold or brave.　　(d) To capitulate

_____

_____

7. (a) seems worse than it really is.　　(c) A permanent problem is one that
   (b) requires attention right away.　　(d) An urgent problem is one that

_____

_____

8. (a) To disrupt a program is to　　(c) be responsible for running it.
   (b) To administer a program is to　　(d) provide the money for it.

_____

_____

adequate
administer
agitate
capitulate
citrus
disrupt
hovel
illiterate
indifferent
menial
permanent
respite
strenuous
toil
urgent

9. (a) A respite is   (c) a lemon or similar fruit.
   (b) A citrus is   (d) a task requiring hard work.

_____

_____

10. (a) that person is disturbed or upset. (c) If someone is agitated,
    (b) that person avoids other people.   (d) If someone is disruptive,

_____

_____

5B ▶ Just the Right Word

Improve each of the following sentences by crossing out the bold phrase and replacing it with a word (or a form of the word) from Word List 5.

1. Although entry-level jobs may seem **low level and humble,** young people can still take pride in them and do them to the best of their ability.

2. Political protesters **stirred up** the crowd with their loud, expressive language.

3. A two-room apartment is **just large enough** for one person.

4. The work of a logger is **tiring because it requires a lot of effort.**

5. The man who was **causing a disturbance** during the performance was asked to be quiet.

6. I'm afraid that this ink stain is **not going to go away.**

7. Although I asked him for help repeatedly, he was **not interested in listening** to my requests.

8. We worked in the garden all afternoon without a **break from our activity.**

9. What an unpleasant task it was to **make my way with difficulty** through 500 pages of small print.

10. This medicine must be **given to the patient** by a nurse or doctor.

Circle the letter or letters of each correct answer. A question may have more than one correct answer.

1. Which of the following would be a matter of **urgency?**
   - (a) a bomb threat
   - (b) a sudden epidemic
   - (c) a hurricane warning
   - (d) an overdue library book

2. Which of the following can become **agitated?**
   - (a) water
   - (b) a crowd
   - (c) a rock
   - (d) a child

3. Which of the following is a **citrus** fruit?
   - (a) a grapefruit
   - (b) an avocado
   - (c) a kumquat
   - (d) a banana

4. Which of the following might an **illiterate** person do?
   - (a) play checkers
   - (b) write a report
   - (c) solve a crossword puzzle
   - (d) play a word game

5. Which of the following can **capitulate?**
   - (a) an army
   - (b) a country
   - (c) a person
   - (d) a building

6. Which of the following is a **strenuous** activity?
   - (a) shoveling snow
   - (b) swimming
   - (c) washing dishes
   - (d) taking a stroll

7. Which of the following can be **disrupted?**
   - (a) a speech
   - (b) a meeting
   - (c) one's education
   - (d) one's vacation

8. Which of the following is an **adequate** grade?
   - (a) A-
   - (b) C+
   - (c) B
   - (d) F

adequate

administer

agitate

capitulate

citrus

disrupt

hovel

illiterate

indifferent

menial

permanent

respite

strenuous

toil

urgent

Complete the analogies by selecting the pair of words whose relationship most resembles the relationship of the pair in capital letters. Circle the letter in front of the pair you choose.

1. INCREASE : SUBSIDE ::
   (a) praise : flatter
   (b) guess : estimate
   (c) lessen : abate
   (d) expand : contract

2. ILLITERATE : READ ::
   (a) immortal : die
   (b) dilapidated : renovate
   (c) urgent : urge
   (d) tired : stumble

3. SURRENDER : CAPITULATE ::
   (a) heed : annihilate
   (b) rest : toil
   (c) arrive : depart
   (d) gain : acquire

4. UPSET : AGHAST ::
   (a) mortal : immortal
   (b) genuine : authentic
   (c) hungry : thirsty
   (d) tired : exhausted

5. HEED : IGNORE ::
   (a) lend : debt
   (b) disturb : agitate
   (c) accept : reject
   (d) maintain : declare

6. HOVEL : PALACE ::
   (a) hut : shelter
   (b) king : queen
   (c) money : health
   (d) poverty : wealth

7. LEMON : CITRUS ::
   (a) apple : orange
   (b) wheat : grain
   (c) letter : package
   (d) plant : animal

8. TOIL : TIRED ::
   (a) devour : full
   (b) judging : impartial
   (c) hiking : devious
   (d) supplies : adequate

9. REPRIMAND : PRAISE ::
   (a) disrupt : interrupt
   (b) correspond : match
   (c) surrender : capitulate
   (d) insult : flatter

10. PERMANENT : TEMPORARY ::
   (a) astute : clever
   (b) abbreviated : brief
   (c) competent : able
   (d) industrious : lazy

Read the passage. Then answer the questions that follow it.

Harvest of Shame

Many Americans are lucky to have ample supplies of fruits and vegetables in their supermarkets twelve months a year. And who picks all this food? More than a million women, children, and men do. They travel the United States picking asparagus and strawberries in Washington state, **citrus** fruits in Florida, apples in New York state, and many kinds of vegetables in California. These laborers are called migrant farm workers because they move from place to place, wherever crops need picking. Most would prefer **permanent** full-time employment, but it is not often available to them.

The work day is **strenuous;** pickers bend and stoop, often under a blazing hot sun. And the day is long—from seven in the morning until seven at night. Their only **respite** may be a twenty-minute lunch break. It is considered **menial** work; wages are low, and laborers are paid only when they pick. If it rains, or if they are too sick to work, they get nothing. What's more, they cannot get **adequate** medical treatment when they are ill or injured.

The children suffer because their education is **disrupted** as they move from school to school. In fact, only one student in ten graduates from high school. The young people often drop out of school altogether to **toil** in the fields alongside their parents. It is there that they may be exposed to chemical pesticides sprayed on crops. One California study showed cancer among migrant workers' children at twelve times the normal rate.

In the 1960s, laborers in California began to **agitate** for better working conditions. The growers were **indifferent** to their demands. So the migrant workers, under the leadership of two Mexican-Americans, Cesar Chavez and Dolores Fernandez Huerta, formed a labor union called the United Farm Workers of America. When growers tried to ignore the union, it called strikes and organized boycotts of California lettuce and grapes. It took years of struggle, many organized marches, and sometimes violent clashes, but in the end most of the growers **capitulated.** In 1966, they recognized the union's right to represent workers.

Despite the union's efforts, conditions have improved only slightly since the 1960s. One notable accomplishment has been the creation of the East Coast Migrant Head Start Project, which **administers** many child-care centers

adequate
administer
agitate
capitulate
citrus
disrupt
hovel
illiterate
indifferent
menial
permanent
respite
strenuous
toil
urgent

for migrants. Started in 1974, by 2002 it operated ninety-two centers in eleven states. Though this helped to improve conditions in some areas, the need for more programs is **urgent.** Educational programs could lower **illiteracy** rates among migrant workers and their families. Outreach programs could also help to improve migrant workers' living conditions. Many workers live without running water and electricity. These necessary additions and minimal repairs to their homes would help to turn them from inadequate **hovels** into acceptable community housing.

In 1960, a film about migrant farm workers aired on television. The film shocked the nation. Sadly, if the film were to be shown today, very little of it would seem out of date. And its title would be as apt today as it was then. The film is called *Harvest of Shame*.

▶ **Answer each of the following questions in the form of a sentence. If a question does not contain a vocabulary word from the lesson's word list, use one in your answer. Use each word only once.**

1. What is the meaning of **strenuous** as it is used in the passage?

_____

_____

2. What do oranges, grapefruit, and lemons have in common?

_____

_____

3. What is the meaning of **administers** as it is used in the passage?

_____

_____

4. Describe the living conditions of many migrant farm workers.

_____

_____

5. In what ways did the farm workers **agitate** for better conditions?

_____

_____

6. Is there still much need to improve the conditions of migrant workers?

_____

_____

7. What is the meaning of **disrupted** as it is used in the passage?

_____

_____

8. Why do some consider this type of work **menial?**

_____

_____

9. What did farm workers gain when the growers **capitulated** in 1966?

_____

_____

10. What is the meaning of **toil** as it is used in the passage?

_____

_____

11. How would **permanent** employment improve the state of migrant workers?

_____

_____

12. Why is a twenty-minute lunch break especially welcome to farm workers?

_____

_____

13. What is the meaning of **indifferent** as it is used in the passage?

_____

_____

14. Why is the produce section at supermarkets usually well stocked?

_____

_____

15. How could educational programs help the workers and their families?

_____

_____

adequate

administer

agitate

capitulate

citrus

disrupt

hovel

illiterate

indifferent

menial

permanent

respite

strenuous

toil

urgent

- The noun formed from the verb **administer** is *administration*; its general meaning is "the management of a business" but it also has a specialized meaning, "the members of the executive branch of government, headed by the president." In this meaning, the word is usually capitalized. (During the Clinton *Administration,* Janet Reno became the first female Attorney General of the United States.) The other two branches of government are the legislative (the Senate and the House of Representatives) and the judicial (headed by the United States Supreme Court).

- The Latin word for *break* is *ruptura;* from it we form the verbs **disrupt** and *interrupt.* If you *interrupt* a speaker, you *break* in on what that person is saying. If you try to *disrupt* a meeting, you are attempting to *break* it up.

- The antonym of **illiterate** is *literate.* Its primary meaning is "able to read," but it has two secondary meanings: "well-read" (a *literate* scholar), and "well-written; polished" (a *literate* essay).

Lesson 6

| Word List | Study the definitions of the words. Then do the exercises that follow. |

addict
ad´ ikt

n. 1. A person with a very strong desire for something that is habit-forming and sometimes harmful.
Junk food **addicts** need to change their eating habits.

2. A person who is a very enthusiastic fan.
A true crossword puzzle **addict** should complete this puzzle in twenty minutes.

v. (ə dikt´) To cause someone to have a very strong desire for something.
Pushers try to **addict** people to illegal drugs.

addiction   *n.* (ə dik´ shən) The condition of being addicted.
We need more treatment centers for drug **addiction.**

addictive   *adj.* (ə dik´ tiv) Likely to cause addiction.
Cocaine is an **addictive** substance.

aspire
ə spīr´

v. To have a strong desire to get or do something; to seek.
Every NFL team **aspires** to win the Super Bowl.

aspiration   *n.* (as pər ā´ shən) A strong desire to achieve something; an ambition.
Jian Xiao sings in local clubs but has **aspirations** to be an opera singer.

bias
bī´ əs

n. A preference that prevents one from being impartial; prejudice.
The lawyers in town insist that Judge Lewis shows **bias** in favor of women.

v. To cause someone to have prejudice; to influence.
Don't let a single bad experience with one French restaurant **bias** you against all others.

blatant
blāt´ nt

adj. Very obvious in an offensive or shameless way.
The governor's promise to cut taxes if re-elected was a **blatant** attempt to win votes.

candid
kan´ did

adj. Expressed honestly and without holding back unpleasant truths.
Tony asked the teacher for her **candid** opinion about his poem.

confront
kən frunt´

v. 1. To stand up to; to face boldly.
Do you intend to **confront** the people who have been spreading rumors about you?

2. To put or bring face to face.
When the police **confronted** the pair with the evidence, they confessed to the robbery.

confrontation *n.* (kän frən tā´shən) A hostile meeting between people who hold opposite views.
Rosie avoided a **confrontation** with her mother by staying in her room.

debut
dā´ byōō

n. A first public appearance.
Radio broadcasting made its **debut** in 1920.

v. To make a first public appearance.
The new television shows **debut** in September.

enroll
en rōl´

v. To sign up to become a member of some group or activity; to register.
A small inheritance made it possible for me to **enroll** in art school.

enrollment *n.* The number of people enrolled.
The karate class has an **enrollment** of six students.

fluster
flus´tər

v. To make nervous, embarrassed, or confused.
The personal question **flustered** me, so I was unable to think of an answer quickly.

impunity
im pyōō´nə tē

n. Freedom from being harmed or punished.
Those who think they can smoke cigarettes with **impunity** are sadly mistaken.

intensify
in ten´sə fī

v. To increase; to strengthen or deepen.
Volunteers will **intensify** their efforts to find the missing children.

intimidate
in tim´ə dāt

v. To frighten, especially by threatening someone.
The pitcher's scowl was intended to **intimidate** the batter.

intimidation *n.* (in tim ə dā´shən) The act of intimidating.
Jones claimed that **intimidation** had been used to make him confess to the crime.

obnoxious
äb näk´shəs

adj. Very unpleasant; disgusting.
An **obnoxious** diner at the next table ruined our meal by complaining in a very loud voice.

retort
rē tôrt´

v. To answer, especially in a quick or clever way.
"You have much to be modest about," I **retorted** when the speaker claimed to be a modest person.

n. A quick or clever reply.
Unable to think of a suitable **retort,** I remained silent.

stint   *n.* 1. A period of time devoted to a job or some task.
stint   After finishing college, Marsha had a two-year **stint** in the Peace Corps in Kenya.

2. A limit or restriction.
Local benefactors gave without **stint** to help make the youth center a reality.

v. To limit or restrict.
Many parents **stint** on luxuries to pay for their children's education.

6A   Finding Meanings

Choose two phrases to form a sentence that correctly uses a word from Word List 6. Write each sentence in the space provided.

1. (a) To debut is to
   (b) overcome difficulties.
   (c) limit or restrict.
   (d) To stint is to

   _____

   _____

2. (a) Impunity is
   (b) Intimidation is
   (c) the act of threatening a person.
   (d) a strong desire to succeed.

   _____

   _____

3. (a) is a habit that is hard to break.
   (b) is a desire to do well.
   (c) An addiction
   (d) A confrontation

   _____

   _____

4. (a) to break a bad habit.
   (b) To debut is
   (c) to make a first public appearance.
   (d) To retort is

   _____

   _____

5. (a) face that person boldly.
   (b) To confront someone is to
   (c) To enroll someone is to
   (d) fail to treat that person fairly.

   _____

   _____

addict

aspire

bias

blatant

candid

confront

debut

enroll

fluster

impunity

intensify

intimidate

obnoxious

retort

stint

6. (a) A candid answer is one   (c) that is made up on the spur of the moment.

    (b) A blatant lie is one   (d) that is obvious to everyone.

_____

_____

7. (a) Bias is   (c) freedom from the fear of punishment.
    (b) Impunity is   (d) the inability to break a habit.

_____

_____

8. (a) An addict is   (c) a clever reply.
    (b) An aspiration is   (d) an enthusiastic fan.

_____

_____

9. (a) does not hold back the truth.   (c) An obnoxious person is one who
    (b) is anxious to please.   (d) A candid person is one who

_____

_____

10. (a) a first public appearance.   (c) a quick and clever reply.
     (b) A retort is   (d) A bias is

_____

_____

6B ▶ Just the Right Word

Improve each of the following sentences by crossing out the bold phrase and replacing it with a word (or a form of the word) from Word List 6.

1. A **definite amount of time spent working** in the kitchen was part of each camper's daily routine.

2. It's best to **face up to** your problems rather than to hope they'll go away.

3. The band made its **first public appearance** precisely one year ago.

4. The smell from the fish processing plant was **not only unpleasant but disgusting,** so the authorities closed the building down.

5. The weather report said that the heat will **become more extreme** as the day wears on.

6. Many comedians who work in clubs have **strong ambitions** to appear on national television.

7. Some people ask you to be **honest in what you say** and then get upset when you are.

8. Those with an **inability to say no** to illegal drugs need treatment rather than punishment.

9. My new year's resolution is to **sign up as a student** in the community center's yoga class.

10. Your **inability to take an impartial position** prevents you from considering both sides of the question.

6c ▶ Applying Meanings

Circle the letter or letters of each correct answer. A question may have more than one correct answer.

addict
aspire
bias
blatant
candid
confront
debut
enroll
fluster
impunity
intensify
intimidate
obnoxious
retort
stint

1. Which of the following cannot be done with **impunity?**
   (a) walking the dog
   (b) neglecting to pay bills
   (c) losing weight
   (d) skipping classes

2. In which of the following might one **enroll?**
   (a) a painting class
   (b) a birthday party
   (c) the Peace Corps
   (d) summer camp

3. To which of the following might one **aspire?**
   (a) the presidency
   (b) a jail sentence
   (c) a career in the theater
   (d) being born to wealthy parents

4. Which of the following can be **intensified?**
   (a) one's efforts
   (b) criticism
   (c) a search
   (d) a number between 1 and 10

5. Which of the following might **intimidate** a person?
   (a) an offer of help
   (c) threat of a reprimand
   (b) a parent's anger
   (d) speaking before a large group

6. Which of the following can be **blatant?**
   (a) a lie
   (c) an insult
   (b) an error
   (d) a secret

7. Which of the following might **fluster** a speaker?
   (a) mixing up his or her notes
   (c) going on past the time allowed
   (b) taunts from the audience
   (d) forgetting the chairperson's name

8. To which of the following can a person become **addicted?**
   (a) soap operas
   (c) horror movies
   (b) alcohol
   (d) cigarettes

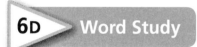

6D Word Study

Each group of four words contains either two synonyms or two antonyms. Circle that pair. Then circle the S if they are synonyms or the A if they are antonyms.

1. blatant	biased	unwanted	impartial	S	A
2. candid	obnoxious	pleasant	silent	S	A
3. reply	aspire	remove	retort	S	A
4. intimidate	stint	increase	scare	S	A
5. candid	devious	addictive	urgent	S	A
6. decrease	enroll	intensify	appear	S	A
7. habit-forming	blatant	unending	addictive	S	A
8. reply	enroll	register	fluster	S	A
9. stint	debut	desire	limit	S	A
10. confront	arrange	fluster	confuse	S	A

Read the passage. Then answer the questions that follow it.

Out of Her League?

Pam Postema grew up in Willard, Ohio, hooked on sports and with an unusual ambition—she **aspired** to be a major-league baseball umpire. At the time, this seemed like an impossible dream. No one took her seriously. Postema persisted, however, and in 1977 **enrolled** in the country's top umpiring school. At that time, she was twenty-two and well aware of the strong **bias** against women in professional baseball. Although the school she chose to attend had previously accepted several women, none had completed the course. In its entire history, the school had graduated seven thousand men but not one woman!

The umpiring school's chief instructor treated Postema fairly, and he was also very **candid** with her. He told her that her chances of getting a top job in the future were slim. In order to make it into the major leagues, she would have to be twice as good as any man. Postema was determined to succeed, and she did well at the school, graduating seventeenth out of a class of over a hundred students. She began at once to look for a job as a professional baseball umpire.

Within a few months, Postema made her professional **debut** with the Gulf Coast Single A League. During the next few years, she advanced steadily. In 1983, she began calling plays in the Triple A Pacific League, one step below the majors. It was not easy, though. If a male umpire made a bad call, it was brushed aside. If Postema did the same thing, she was accused of becoming **flustered.** Some baseball fans seized on any errors she made as "proof" that umpiring was not an appropriate occupation for a woman.

Postema believed that a manager would often view a **confrontation** with her as a test of his manhood; if he failed to **intimidate** her, he felt somehow disgraced. She wanted to show that no one should expect to attack her authority with **impunity,** so she ejected managers and players from the game at twice the rate of other umpires. She even had three spectators thrown out of the ballpark for making **obnoxious** remarks about female umpires. Postema admits she sometimes enjoyed arguing, whether with managers, players, or even other umpires. In fact, she says that many umpires are **addicted** to arguing.

addict

aspire

bias

blatant

candid

confront

debut

enroll

fluster

impunity

intensify

intimidate

obnoxious

retort

stint

In 1988, Postema got a job umpiring the National League spring-training games, where she had to deal with major-league players and managers. When the starting pitcher for the Pittsburgh Pirates told a reporter that God never intended women to be major-league baseball umpires, Postema **retorted** that she doubted that God was interested in baseball. Not everyone was as **blatant** as the Pirates' pitcher. But the hostility directed against her, far from diminishing, seemed to **intensify** as her career advanced.

Pam Postema's career as a professional baseball umpire was marked by talent and spirit. Her **stint** in the minors had lasted seven years when she was dropped from the official list of umpires. There was nothing unusual about this. After about five years in the minors, most umpires are let go to give others a chance; very few make it into the majors.

▶ **Answer each of the following questions in the form of a sentence. If a question does not contain a vocabulary word from the lesson's word list, use one in your answer. Use each word only once.**

1. When did Pam Postema make her first professional public appearance in a major-league game?

_____

_____

2. Did Postema fulfill her chief **aspiration?**

_____

_____

3. How did Postema show that managers could not easily **intimidate** her?

_____

_____

4. According to Postema, what habit is often common in umpires?

_____

_____

5. Why was it especially important for Postema not to get **flustered?**

_____

_____

6. How did three fans learn early on that they couldn't insult Postema with **impunity?**

_____

_____

7. What happens to most minor-league umpires?

_____

_____

8. Why might Postema have had reason to respect her instructor's predictions about her future in the major leagues?

_____

_____

9. Was Postema the first woman to attend the umpiring school?

_____

_____

10. How did the Pirates' pitcher show his **bias?**

_____

_____

11. Was the remark of the Pirates' pitcher typical of other pitchers as well?

_____

_____

12. How did Postema feel about sexist remarks from spectators?

_____

_____

13. Who had the last word in the argument between Postema and the Pirates' pitcher?

_____

_____

14. According to Postema, why did managers often make life difficult for her?

_____

_____

addict
aspire
bias
blatant
candid
confront
debut
enroll
fluster
impunity
intensify
intimidate
obnoxious
retort
stint

15. How did Postema demonstrate that she was not a quitter?

_____

_____

FUN & FASCINATING FACTS

- The English word **candid** comes from the Latin verb *candere,* which means "to shine." Truth is like a light, sometimes exposing what someone might wish to hide. A *candid* person shines the light of truth on something others might wish to conceal.

- The Latin verb *punire* means "to punish" and forms the root of several other English words besides *punish* and **impunity.** If a jury awards *punitive* damages to someone who has been injured, the intention is to punish those who caused the injury. If you pay a *penalty,* you are being punished for doing what you shouldn't have done or for failing to do what you should have done. A state's *penal* system is designed to punish criminals by putting them in jail.

- **Obnoxious** is formed from the Latin *noxa,* meaning "an injury"; so is *noxious,* meaning "harmful" or "unhealthy" (*noxious* gas from car exhaust). The smell from a skunk is *obnoxious* but not *noxious.* Carbon monoxide gas is *noxious* but not *obnoxious* (because it cannot be smelled). Cigarette smoke is *noxious;* it is also *obnoxious* to non-smokers who are sometimes forced to inhale it when someone near them is smoking.

For more practice and games, go to www.WordlyWise3000.com.

Word List	Study the definitions of the words. Then do the exercises that follow.

beseech
bē sēch´

v. To ask earnestly; to beg.
I **beseech** you to stay just one more day.

consternation
kän stər na´ shən

n. Amazement or fear that makes one feel confused.
We were filled with **consternation** when we saw that our car had been towed.

delectable
dē lek´ tə bəl

adj. Pleasing to the senses, especially to the sense of taste; delicious.
My grandfather's homemade apple pie is **delectable.**

garland
gär´ lənd

n. A wreath or chain of leaves and flowers.
The islanders greet new arrivals with **garlands** of fresh flowers to put around their necks.

gratify
grat´ i fī

v. 1. To please or satisfy.
The Red Cross was **gratified** by the response to its appeal for blood donors.

2. To give in to what is wanted or requested.
My parents were unable to **gratify** my wish for a pony.

gratifying *adj.* Pleasing.
It is **gratifying** to see one's hard work in math rewarded with higher grades.

haughty
hôt´ ē

adj. Showing too much pride in oneself and scorn or contempt for others.
The supervisor's **haughty** manner made her unpopular in the office.

haughtiness *n.* The state or quality of being haughty.
His **haughtiness** seemed absurd for one who had accomplished so little.

impetuous
im pech´ ōō əs

adj. Inclined to act without thinking; hasty.
I regretted my **impetuous** decision to invite everyone at Marcello's party to come over to my place.

lavish
lav´ ish

adj. 1. Much more than enough.
The Chinese New Year's celebration included a **lavish** fifteen-course meal.

2. Very costly.
The tribal chiefs at the ceremony bestowed **lavish** gifts on each other as signs of respect.

v. To give freely or generously.
Critics **lavished** praise on the new Broadway musical.

pluck
pluk

v. 1. To pull off or out; to pick.
I was tempted to **pluck** a rose from the bush, but the sight of the thorns stopped me.

2. To remove the feathers from.
This machine can **pluck** a chicken in less than eight seconds.

3. To pull at and let go.
You play the harp by **plucking** the strings gently.

n. Courage; bravery.
It took a lot of **pluck** for Rico to learn to walk again.

plucky *adj.* Brave; courageous.
After a **plucky** attempt to rescue the kitten stuck in the tree, Monique had to call the fire department.

ponder
pän´dər

v. To think about; to consider carefully.
Lost in thought, the chess player **pondered** her next move.

privilege
priv´ə lij

n. A special favor, right, or advantage given to a person or group.
Free parking at Reagan National Airport is one of the **privileges** enjoyed by members of Congress.

privileged *adj.* Given favors or advantages denied to others.
You should feel **privileged** that you were able to attend an Ivy League school.

prostrate
präs´trāt

adj. 1. Lying flat.
Having fainted, he lay **prostrate** on the floor.

2. Lying facedown, especially to show respect.
The worshippers in the temple lay **prostrate** before the high priest.

3. Completely overcome; weak and helpless.
People were **prostrate** with terror as the tornado approached.

rapture
rap´chər

n. A state of great joy, delight, or love.
The Scot was filled with **rapture** at the sound of bagpipes.

revelry
rev´əl rē

n. Noisy merrymaking.
Sounds of **revelry** came from the locker room after the game.

whim
wim

n. A sudden wish to do something without a particular reason; a fanciful idea.
Purchasing a puppy is not something to be done on a **whim.**

Choose two phrases to form a sentence that correctly uses a word from Word List 7. Write each sentence in the space provided.

1. (a) A plucky attempt is one   (c) An impetuous attempt is one
   (b) that takes a lot of courage.   (d) that is bound to fail.

   _____

   _____

2. (a) To be prostrate is to be   (c) To be gratified is to be
   (b) devoid of hope.   (d) lying with the face downward.

   _____

   _____

3. (a) To act impetuously is to   (c) do something knowing it to be wrong.
   (b) do something without thinking. (d) To act in a haughty manner is to

   _____

   _____

4. (a) is to be watchful and alert.   (c) To be in a state of rapture
   (b) is to be blissfully happy.   (d) To be in a state of consternation

   _____

   _____

5. (a) A haughty person is   (c) one who tries to please others.
   (b) A privileged person is   (d) one who shows contempt for others.

   _____

   _____

6. (a) A whim is   (c) A garland is
   (b) a wreath of leaves and flowers. (d) a small gift.

   _____

   _____

7. (a) Consternation is   (c) Revelry is
   (b) contempt for the feelings   (d) a state of shocked surprise.
       of others.

   _____

   _____

8. (a) To be prostrate is to be   (c) dissatisfied.
   (b) To be gratified is to be   (d) helpless.

   _____

   _____

beseech
consternation
delectable
garland
gratify
haughty
impetuous
lavish
pluck
ponder
privilege
prostrate
rapture
revelry
whim

9. (a) Pluck is   (c) noisy merrymaking.
   (b) a display of joy.   (d) Revelry is

_____

_____

10. (a) to give it freely.   (c) To ponder something is
    (b) To lavish something is   (d) to feel uncomfortable about it.

_____

_____

7B ▶ Just the Right Word

Improve each of the following sentences by crossing out the bold phrase and replacing it with a word (or a form of the word) from Word List 7.

1. I **am making an earnest request to** you not to get involved in their quarrel.

2. The **feeling of great joy and love** in the faces of the bride and groom was captured in the wedding photographs.

3. Imagine being able to buy a plane ticket to Tahiti on a **sudden wish to do something out of the ordinary!**

4. Parents do not have to **show they care by giving in to** every wish of their children.

5. I felt **that I was being given a special favor** when my parents let me borrow the car for the first time.

6. Getting back on a horse after taking a bad fall takes **a lot of courage.**

7. The student **gave a great deal of thought to** the question before replying.

8. The pizza at Saracino's is **pleasing to the taste.**

9. The new government offices are so **much more luxurious than is necessary** that reporters were shocked at the waste of taxpayers' money.

10. We were **lying stretched out flat on the ground** from fatigue after our hike.

Circle the letter or letters of each correct answer. A question may have more than one correct answer.

1. Which of the following can express **haughtiness?**
   (a) a look
   (b) an insult
   (c) a retort
   (d) an epidemic

2. Which of the following could be considered a **privilege?**
   (a) receiving a reprimand
   (b) voting in an election
   (c) staying up late
   (d) paying taxes

3. Which of the following can be **plucked?**
   (a) feathers
   (b) flowers
   (c) trees
   (d) guitar strings

4. Which of the following might be a part of **revelry?**
   (a) dancing
   (b) music
   (c) solitude
   (d) laughter

5. Which of the following actions by children would **gratify** their parents?
   (a) making derogatory remarks
   (b) making astute comments
   (c) cleaning up their rooms
   (d) disrupting supper

6. Which of the following might cause **consternation?**
   (a) losing the car keys
   (b) losing a wallet
   (c) suddenly gaining weight
   (d) suddenly losing weight

7. Which of the following might a person **ponder?**
   (a) a choice of college
   (b) a choice of leader
   (c) the origin of the universe
   (d) braking to avoid an accident

8. Which of the following might be done on a **whim?**
   (a) electing a president
   (b) administering a test
   (c) buying a new coat
   (d) building a space station

beseech
consternation
delectable
garland
gratify
haughty
impetuous
lavish
pluck
ponder
privilege
prostrate
rapture
revelry
whim

The most common meaning of the prefix *in-* is "not" or "without." With this meaning, it turns a word into its opposite. For example, it turns *correct* into *incorrect*. The prefix *in-* can also act as an intensifier, making the word to which it is attached stronger or more emphatic.

To make certain words easier to say, the prefix changes to *im-* before the letters *b*, *m*, and *p*. It changes to *il-* before the letter *l*, and it changes to *ir-* before the letter *r*.

Add the correct form of this prefix to the words. Then write the letter of the definition that best fits each new word.

1. _____precise   _____   a. neither good or bad

2. _____partial   _____   b. not regular

3. _____furiate   _____   c. not relevant

4. _____relevant   _____   d. not precise

5. _____capable   _____   e. very hasty

6. _____different   _____   f. not literate

7. _____lustrious   _____   g. not partial

8. _____petuous   _____   h. not capable

9. _____literate   _____   i. extremely outstanding

10. _____regular   _____   j. make very angry

Read the passage. Then answer the questions that follow it.

The Midas Touch

It is sometimes said of people who are good at making money that everything they touch turns to gold. Such people are said to have "the Midas touch," an expression that comes from an ancient Greek myth.

The Greek god Dionysus was visiting Phrygia, now part of Turkey, when his companion Silenus wandered off and got lost, arriving some time later at the court of King Midas. Having had too much to drink, he slipped off his donkey and fell asleep on the ground. When King Midas came upon him, he recognized Silenus at once and felt **privileged** to receive a visit from the friend of a god.

King Midas was determined to make his guest's stay a pleasant one. Midas's daughter presented Silenus with **garlands** made from flowers she herself had picked. Slaves fell **prostrate** to the ground when he passed and rushed to obey his every **whim.** Musicians filled the air with sweet music wherever he went. And every night the king honored Silenus with a **lavish** banquet at which the most **delectable** dishes were served. In short, Midas did everything he could think of to **gratify** his guest. The **revelries** continued until Dionysus finally arrived in search of his companion.

Dionysus told Midas that in return for his kindness to Silenus, he could have anything he wanted. Now King Midas loved gold almost as much as he loved his own daughter, so he did not stop to **ponder** Dionysus's offer. "Make everything I touch turn to gold," he said. When Dionysus suggested that Midas was being **impetuous,** the king **haughtily** rejected the suggestion. He was too proud to take advice from anyone, even a god. He refused to change his mind, and so Dionysus granted him his wish.

Eager to try out his new power, King Midas rushed into the garden as soon as his visitors had left and **plucked** an apple from a tree. In an instant it turned to gold. The king was in a state of **rapture.** He called out to his daughter and flung his arms around her as he told her the good news. To his **consternation,** she instantly turned into a gold statue.

beseech

consternation

delectable

garland

gratify

haughty

impetuous

lavish

pluck

ponder

privilege

prostrate

rapture

revelry

whim

King Midas was aghast when he saw the consequences of his greed. He **beseeched** Dionysus to take back his gift. Dionysus agreed to do so, and he also restored the king's daughter to her human state. As for King Midas, he learned this important lesson: be careful what you ask for; you might get it.

▶ **Answer each of the following questions in the form of a sentence. If a question does not contain a vocabulary word from the lesson's word list, use one in your answer. Use each word only once.**

1. What is the meaning of **gratify** as it is used in the passage?

_____

_____

2. What brought Midas's **rapture** to an end?

_____

_____

3. Where do you think Midas's daughter placed the **garlands** she gave Silenus?

_____

_____

4. Why might Silenus have praised the chefs who worked for Midas?

_____

_____

5. What is the meaning of **prostrate** as it is used in the passage?

_____

_____

6. How did Midas react when Dionysus suggested that he be cautious?

_____

_____

7. How did Midas's mood change when he saw what he had done?

_____

_____

8. Why should Midas have **pondered** Dionysus's offer?

_____

_____

9. Why did Dionysus agree to take back his gift?

_____

_____

10. What is the meaning of **plucked** as it is used in the passage?

_____

_____

11. Why did Midas go to such trouble to entertain Silenus?

_____

_____

12. Why had Silenus no cause to complain about the service he received?

_____

_____

13. Why did Midas not give himself time to think over Dionysus's offer?

_____

_____

14. For how long did Midas entertain Silenus?

_____

_____

15. What is the meaning of **lavish** as it is used in the passage?

_____

_____

beseech

consternation

delectable

garland

gratify

haughty

impetuous

lavish

pluck

ponder

privilege

prostrate

rapture

revelry

whim

- The adjectives **prostrate** and *prone* both mean "lying with the face downward," but there is a difference between them that should be noted. *Prostrate* suggests either a show of respect or a state of helplessness. *Prone* is a more neutral term; it indicates bodily position and nothing more (lying *prone* in a bed). The antonym of *prone* is *supine;* it means "lying with the face upward."

- The Latin verb *rapere* means "to seize" and forms the root of several English words. To be in a state of **rapture** is to be seized by deep feelings of joy. The adjective *rapt* means "deeply absorbed." It is difficult to get the attention of people who are rapt in thought; it is as though their minds have been seized by thoughts that mentally disconnect them from what is going on around them. Finally, there is *raptor,* the name for a bird of prey that seizes small animals or fish in its talons and carries them off to eat later. Hawks and eagles are raptors.

- In the eighteenth and nineteenth centuries, *whim-wham* was the name for a fanciful or amusing object worn as an ornament or decoration. The origin of the term is unknown, but it became shortened to **whim,** and its meaning was broadened so that a whim came to mean "a fanciful or amusing idea." *Whimsy* is a related word; it means "a fanciful or amusing quality." (The Uncle Remus stories of Joel Chandler Harris are filled with *whimsy*.) The adjective form of *whimsy* is *whimsical;* it means "marked by whimsy; amusing or fanciful." (A battery-powered fork for twirling spaghetti was one of the *whimsical* objects on display.)

Lesson 8

| **Word List** | Study the definitions of the words. Then do the exercises that follow. |

acrid
ak´ rid

adj. Sharp, irritating, or bitter to the sense of taste or smell.
Burning rubber gives off **acrid** fumes.

casualty
kazh´ ōō əl tē

n. A person killed or injured in a war or accident.
There were many **casualties** of the 2011 tsunami, or tidal wave, that struck Japan.

congested
kən jest´ əd

adj. 1. Overcrowded; filled too full.
We take the subway during rush hour to avoid the **congested** city streets.

2. Filled with fluid.
My sinuses get **congested** when the pollen count is high.

congestion *n.* 1. The condition of being overcrowded.
The **congestion** inside the furniture store is due to the "Going out of Business" sale.

2. The condition of being filled with fluid.
Most cold remedies claim to relieve **congestion** for at least eight hours.

cope
kōp

v. To manage problems or difficulties successfully.
Extra police were on duty to **cope** with the large crowds expected for the parade.

headlong
hed´ lôŋ

adj. With great speed or force; reckless.
The crowd made a **headlong** rush for the best seats as soon as the doors were opened.

adv. Recklessly; without time for careful thought.
It's foolish to rush **headlong** into a dispute that doesn't concern you.

hurtle
hərt´ l

v. To move with great force and speed.
A snowball **hurtled** past my ear.

impede
im pēd´

v. To get in the way of; to interfere with the movement of.
An overturned truck **impeded** the flow of traffic.

impediment *n.* (im ped´ ə mənt) An obstacle; something that gets in the way.
Poor roads are an **impediment** to travel.

inevitable
in ev´ ə tə bəl

adj. Bound to happen; unavoidable.
A certain amount of wear on even the best tires is **inevitable** with normal use.

initiate
i nish´ ē āt

v. 1. To put into effect; to bring into use.
The school **initiated** the new dress code on September 6.

2. To take in as a member.
The National Honor Society **initiated** thirty new members last evening.

initiation *n.* (i nish ē ā´ shən) 1. The act of beginning.
The **initiation** of the new traffic plan has been delayed until the road is repaired.

2. The ceremony or process that makes one a member.
A celebration followed the **initiation** of new members into the San Francisco Film Society.

irate
ī rāt´

adj. Very angry; furious.
Irate citizens demanded that the chemical company stop polluting the lake.

lax
laks

adj. 1. Not strictly enforced; undemanding; careless.
Frequent inspections are designed to ensure that airline safety procedures have not become **lax.**

2. Not tight; loose.
When I felt the rope go **lax,** I knew that my partner had dropped the other end.

negligent
neg´ lə jənt

adj. Failing to take proper care of or to give proper attention to.
You were **negligent** in failing to lock the car doors.

negligence *n.* The quality, state, or act of being negligent.
When I went on vacation, my houseplants died because of my roommate's **negligence.**

smolder
smōl´ dər

v. 1. To burn slowly without bursting into flames.
Hot ashes **smolder** long after the flames have died down.

2. To exist in a hidden state before bursting into the open.
A desire for freedom **smoldered** in the hearts of the people who left Cuba for Miami.

stringent
strin´ jənt

adj. Strict; severe.
The **stringent** rules state that no exceptions can be made.

throng
thrôŋ

n. A large number of people gathered together; a crowd.
A **throng** of supporters cheered the president's arrival in Seattle.

v. To gather or move in large numbers.
Fans **thronged** into the ballpark for the first game of the World Series.

Choose two phrases to form a sentence that correctly uses a word from Word List 8. Write each sentence in the space provided.

1. (a) Initiation is
   (b) Negligence is
   (c) a ceremony welcoming new members.
   (d) unnecessary waste.

_____

_____

2. (a) fail to pay proper attention.
   (b) feel desire without showing it.
   (c) To smolder is to
   (d) To hurtle is to

_____

_____

3. (a) Negligence is
   (b) a state of nervousness or fear.
   (c) Congestion is
   (d) the lack of proper attention.

_____

_____

4. (a) gives off an irritating smell.
   (b) burns rapidly.
   (c) Something that is stringent
   (d) Something that is acrid

_____

_____

5. (a) be prostrate with grief.
   (b) To be congested is to
   (c) be filled with fluid.
   (d) To be lax is to

_____

_____

6. (a) A headlong rush is one that
   (b) An inevitable rush is one that
   (c) could have been prevented.
   (d) is bound to happen.

_____

_____

7. (a) To impede a new set of rules
   (b) To cope with a new set of rules
   (c) is to deal successfully with them.
   (d) is to introduce them.

_____

_____

8. (a) A casualty is
   (b) an accident causing death or injury.
   (c) something that holds one back.
   (d) An impediment is

_____

_____

acrid

casualty

congested

cope

headlong

hurtle

impede

inevitable

initiate

irate

lax

negligent

smolder

stringent

throng

9. (a) A headlong exit is one   (c) An irate reply is one
   (b) that is made in a great hurry.   (d) that should not have been made.

_____

_____

10. (a) a person who is killed or injured. (c) A casualty is
    (b) a member of a group.   (d) A throng is

_____

_____

8B ▶ Just the Right Word

Improve each of the following sentences by crossing out the bold phrase and replacing it with a word (or a form of the word) from Word List 8.

1. Changing schools in midyear is difficult, but I'm sure you will **be able to deal successfully with your new situation.**

2. Travelers had to cope with **great numbers of slowly moving vehicles** on the highway over the Labor Day weekend.

3. The bank's rules are so **strictly enforced** that managers have very little latitude when making loans.

4. The garage was found **to have failed to take proper care** in repairing the car's brakes, so it was held responsible for the accident.

5. The voters were **extremely angry** when the governor broke a promise not to raise taxes.

6. A huge rock **moved with great speed and force** down the mountainside.

7. School discipline was **not strictly enforced;** as a result, students' grades suffered.

8. Crowds **were present in large numbers at** the airport to greet the Olympic team.

9. A sailboat ran aground and **got in the way of** the other vessels.

10. Make sure the campfire is out, or it will continue to **burn even though it may not actually burst into flame.**

Applying Meanings

Circle the letter or letters of each correct answer. A question may have more than one correct answer.

1. Which of the following can suffer from **congestion?**
   - (a) city streets
   - (b) a theater lobby
   - (c) a car
   - (d) the passages in one's nose

2. Which of the following can be **initiated?**
   - (a) a new member
   - (b) a new project
   - (c) a new rule
   - (d) a new year

3. Which of the following can **throng?**
   - (a) a pair of horses
   - (b) a pile of stones
   - (c) a flock of seagulls
   - (d) a crowd of people

4. Which of the following often result in **casualties?**
   - (a) a plane crash
   - (b) a wrestling match
   - (c) a war
   - (d) an earthquake

5. Which of the following can **smolder?**
   - (a) a fire
   - (b) anger
   - (c) resentment
   - (d) a flood

6. Which of the following can be **lax?**
   - (a) a metal bar
   - (b) a fishing line
   - (c) supervision
   - (d) rules

7. Which of the following could **hurtle** through the air?
   - (a) a jet fighter
   - (b) a baseball
   - (c) a falling rock
   - (d) a snowflake

8. Which of the following is **inevitable?**
   - (a) growing older
   - (b) getting sick
   - (c) increased world population
   - (d) change in our daily lives

acrid
casualty
congested
cope
headlong
hurtle
impede
inevitable
initiate
irate
lax
negligent
smolder
stringent
throng

Read these Latin words and their meanings. Then fill in the blank spaces in the sentences. The vocabulary words are from this lesson or earlier lessons.

aspirare (to climb)   *delectare* (to delight)   *initium* (beginning)
ira (anger)   *laxus* (loose)   *littera* (letter)
novus (new)   *noxa* (injury)   *poena* (punishment)
stringere (to tie or bind)

1. _____ rules are loosely enforced. The word comes from the Latin
   _____, meaning _____.

2. A _____ item is one that pleases the sense of taste. The word
   comes from the Latin _____, meaning _____.

3. A _____ substance is one that can damage your health. The word
   comes from the Latin _____, meaning _____.

4. To act with _____ is to act without fear of being punished. The
   word comes from the Latin _____, meaning _____.

5. An _____ customer is one who is very angry. The word comes from
   the Latin _____, meaning _____.

6. To _____ a new system is to start using it. The word comes from the
   Latin _____, meaning _____.

7. To _____ a building is to make it like new again. The word comes
   from the Latin _____, meaning _____.

8. An _____ person is one who is unfamiliar with how the letters
   of the alphabet are used. The word comes from the Latin _____,
   meaning _____.

9. A _____ budget is one that is tightly controlled. The word comes
   from the Latin _____, meaning _____.

10. To _____ to a career in acting is to have a strong desire for it. The
    word comes from the Latin _____, meaning _____.

Read the passage. Then answer the questions that follow it.

The Triangle Fire

A hundred years ago, American industry was growing fast and needed workers badly. It found them in the millions of immigrants who poured into the United States from Europe. Most passed through Ellis Island in New York Harbor with little money and few possessions. Many went no farther than New York City in their search for jobs. Young women found employment in the overcrowded, unsanitary, and unsafe factories of the city's garment district. In these sweatshops they worked long hours for low wages. Fire inspections were **lax,** and fire equipment was inadequate. It was **inevitable** that tragedy would strike sooner or later.

On Saturday, March 25, 1911, the top three floors of a ten-story building on New York's Lower East Side were crowded with women working for the Triangle Shirtwaist Company. Late in the afternoon, a bin containing waste fabric on the eighth floor began to **smolder.** No one noticed until it suddenly burst into flames. Women in the crowded workroom tried frantically to put out the rapidly spreading fire. Their efforts were in vain. **Acrid** smoke filled the room. Many of the women, coughing, choking, and unable to see where they were going, were trampled in the **headlong** rush for the only unlocked door in the workroom. The owners of the company always kept the other doors locked; that was to prevent women from slipping outside into the hallway for a break when they were supposed to be working.

Those who fled into the heavily **congested** hallway found that just one elevator was working; only twelve women were able to use it. The fire escape collapsed under the weight of people crowding onto it. The narrow stairway, less than three feet wide, **impeded** the movement of the women, leaving many trapped. More than forty women jumped from windows and **hurtled** to their deaths eighty-five feet below; others flung themselves down the elevator shaft in desperate attempts to escape. Firefighters at the scene were unable to **cope** with the situation. Water from their hoses failed to reach the flames because the pressure was too low; their ladders reached only to the sixth floor.

acrid
casualty
congested
cope
headlong
hurtle
impede
inevitable
initiate
irate
lax
negligent
smolder
stringent
throng

A **throng** estimated at over a hundred thousand people attended the mass funeral of the victims of the fire. Incredible as it sounds, an official inquiry later found that the Triangle Shirtwaist Company had not been guilty of **negligence. Irate** citizens demanded that such a tragedy never be allowed to happen again; and, as a result of the fire, new safety measures were **initiated.** Laws dealing with building safety were made more **stringent,** and firefighting equipment and methods were improved. But the changes came too late for the unfortunate 145 women who were **casualties** of New York's Triangle fire.

▶ **Answer each of the following questions in the form of a sentence. If a question does not contain a vocabulary word from the lesson's word list, use one in your answer. Use each word only once.**

1. Why did the fleeing women have trouble breathing?

_____

_____

2. What happened to the women who jumped from the windows?

_____

_____

3. What was the number of victims of the Triangle fire?

_____

_____

4. What is the meaning of **lax** as it is used in the passage?

_____

_____

5. Did anything good result from the Triangle fire?

_____

_____

6. What did the official inquiry fail to do?

_____

_____

7. Why were the citizens of New York **irate?**

_____

_____

8. What is the meaning of **smolder** as it is used in the passage?

_____

_____

9. How did the narrowness of the stairway contribute to the disaster?

_____

_____

10. Did the women leave the work area in an orderly manner?

_____

_____

11. How did their inadequate equipment hamper the firefighters?

_____

_____

12. What is the meaning of **congested** as it is used in the passage?

_____

_____

13. What is the meaning of **initiated** as it is used in the passage?

_____

_____

14. How did the people of New York pay their respects to the dead women?

_____

_____

15. What was so terrible about the lack of concern by the authorities?

_____

_____

acrid
casualty
congested
cope
headlong
hurtle
impede
inevitable
initiate
irate
lax
negligent
smolder
stringent
throng

- **Initiate** and *begin* are synonyms, but their meanings carry a difference that should be noted. *Begin* is the general, all-purpose word for the start of something; one can *begin* anything from a sentence to a world war! *Initiate* has a narrower meaning; it suggests taking the first in a series of major steps. (A president may *initiate* a new trade policy; a company may *initiate* new hiring practices.)

Initiative is the first step in bringing something about. (I took the *initiative* by demanding a change.)

Initiative is also the ability to get things done without waiting to be told. (You must show *initiative* if you wish to be promoted.)

- **Negligent** means "failing to give proper attention to" and is formed from the verb *neglect*. Another adjective, *negligible,* is formed from this verb; it means "so small or unimportant that it can be neglected or ignored." (The cost of floor mats was *negligible* compared to the price of the car.)

Crossword Puzzle

Solve the crossword puzzle by studying the clues and filling in the answer boxes. Clues followed by a number are definitions of words in Lessons 5 through 8. The number gives the word list in which the answer to the clue appears.

Clues Across

1. Expressed honestly and without holding back (6)
7. To burn slowly without bursting into flame (8)
8. Relating to work requiring little skill (5)
9. Short for Peter
10. To think about carefully (7)
11. A period of rest (5)
13. To give freely and generously (7)
14. Needing to be attended to at once (5)
15. To ask earnestly (7)
17. Courage; bravery (7)
20. Opposite of front
21. To gather or move in large numbers (8)
22. Remain
24. To work long and hard (5)
25. To stir up interest in a cause (5)
26. Failing to pay proper attention to (8)

Clues Down

2. Just enough; sufficient (5)
3. Very angry (8)
4. Amazement or dismay that causes confusion (7)
5. Opposite of rear
6. Relating to oranges, lemons, and similar fruits (5)
9. A special favor given to a person or a group (7)
11. Noisy merrymaking (7)
12. A first public appearance (6)
15. A showing of an unfair preference (6)
16. To move with great force and speed (8)
18. The Grand _____ is in Arizona.
19. An unpleasant and cramped place to live (5)
23. Two sides pull on a rope in a _____ of war.

For more practice and games, go to www.WordlyWise3000.com.

Word List

Study the definitions of the words. Then do the exercises that follow.

dumbfound
dum´ found

v. To make speechless with amazement.
The announcement that my cat Patch had won "best of show" **dumbfounded** me.

dumbfounded *adj.* Speechless with amazement.
The **dumbfounded** tenants stared at the eviction notice in disbelief.

ensue
en soo´

v. To follow; to come as a result of or at a later time.
When the headmaster declared the next day a holiday, shouting and clapping **ensued.**

era
er´ ə

n. A particular period in history.
The **era** of space exploration began in the 1950s.

flourish
flʊr´ ish

v. 1. To thrive or prosper.
Plants **flourish** in a greenhouse.

2. To wave in the air.
The softball player **flourished** her hat above her head to acknowledge the crowd's cheers.

n. 1. A sweeping motion.
The star of the show made her first entrance with a **flourish.**

2. A showy burst of music.
The opera begins with a **flourish** of trumpets.

3. A fancy line or curve added to something written.
His artistic nature was expressed in the **flourish** with which he signed his name.

garrison
gar´ ə sən

n. 1. Soldiers stationed in a place to protect it.
The **garrison** held off the enemy for four days before capitulating.

2. A military place of protection, together with its soldiers and weapons.
The **garrison** controlled the only passage through the mountain range.

v. To provide soldiers with a place to live.
The commander had to **garrison** the troops in an old schoolhouse.

grievous
grē´ vəs

adj. Causing grief or pain; hard to bear.
It was a **grievous** loss to the entire family when our pet dog Tiny died.

hoard hôrd	*v.* To save and put away, especially secretly. Squirrels **hoard** acorns for the winter. *n.* Anything put away in such a manner. My **hoard** of comic books includes several authentic 1930s Superman comics.
inundate in´ ən dāt	*v.* 1. To cover, as with water from a flood. The valley was **inundated** when the dam burst. 2. To load with an excessive amount or number of something. Fans **inundated** radio stations with requests to play the Wailers' new album.
invincible in vin´ sə bəl	*adj.* Impossible to defeat. When the Yankees had a fifteen-game winning streak, we began to think they were **invincible.**
nomad nō´ mad	*n.* A member of a group that settles briefly in one place and then moves on to another. The Bedouins of the Sahara and Arabian deserts were **nomads.** **nomadic** *adj.* (nō mad´ ik) Having the characteristics of a nomad. After acquiring horses in the 1760s, the Cheyenne became **nomadic** buffalo hunters on the Great Plains.
placate plā´ kāt	*v.* To stop from being angry; to calm. I was able to **placate** my friend when I explained my reason for being late.
principal prin´ sə pəl	*adj.* Most important. The administration's **principal** objective is to reduce the school dropout rate. *n.* 1. A person or thing that is of the greatest importance. The club owners and the players' agent are the **principals** in the dispute over baseball players' salaries. 2. The head of a school. The **principal** has the authority to hire extra teachers if student enrollment increases. 3. The sum of money owed, not including the interest. You would need $8,479 to pay off the **principal** on the car loan.
recede ri sēd´	*v.* 1. To move back or to drop to a lower level. The tide **receded** and exposed the rocks near the shore. 2. To become fainter. The blare of the music from the car's radio **receded** as it disappeared into the night.
ruthless rōōth´ ləs	*adj.* Showing no mercy; pitiless. Disease and inadequate supplies finally terminated the **ruthless** invader Attila the Hun in fifth-century Europe.

sacrifice

sak´ rə fis

n. 1. Something given up for the sake of another.
The parents made many **sacrifices** so that their children could go to college.

2. An offering to a god.
In the Incan culture, **sacrifices** were often made during or after an earthquake, drought, or epidemic.

v. 1. To give up something for another.
I **sacrificed** my privacy by sharing my room with my sister.

2. To offer something of value to a god.
Goats and dogs were **sacrificed** at the ancient Roman festival of Lupercalia.

9A ▷ **Finding Meanings**

Choose two phrases to form a sentence that correctly uses a word from Word List 9. Write each sentence in the space provided.

1. (a) A flourish is
   (b) a burst of music.
   (c) A garrison is
   (d) a troubling situation.

   _____

   _____

2. (a) A principal is
   (b) an exchange for something else.
   (c) A hoard is
   (d) a collection put away secretly.

   _____

   _____

3. (a) speechless with amazement.
   (b) To be grievous is to be
   (c) To be inundated is to be
   (d) covered with water.

   _____

   _____

4. (a) provide them with a place to live.
   (b) To sacrifice soldiers is to
   (c) try to satisfy their demands.
   (d) To garrison soldiers is to

   _____

   _____

5. (a) a sum of money owed.
   (b) a truth by which we govern ourselves.
   (c) Principal is
   (d) A nomad is

   _____

   _____

6. (a) calm that person.   (c) To placate someone is to
   (b) To dumbfound someone is to   (d) show that person no mercy.

   _____

   _____

7. (a) prevented from moving.   (c) speechless with amazement.
   (b) To be dumbfounded is to be   (d) To be invincible is to be

   _____

   _____

8. (a) An era is   (c) a burst of music that announces
                        an arrival.
   (b) A sacrifice is   (d) something that is given up for another.

   _____

   _____

9. (a) lack the means to support   (c) Ruthless people are those who
   themselves.
   (b) keep moving from place to place. (d) Nomadic people are those who

   _____

   _____

10. (a) a person of the greatest   (c) A flourish is
    importance.
    (b) An era is   (d) a sweeping motion.

    _____

    _____

11. (a) A ruthless person is one who   (c) exists only in stories.
    (b) An invincible person is one who (d) cannot be defeated.

    _____

    _____

dumbfound

ensue

era

flourish

garrison

grievous

hoard

inundate

invincible

nomad

placate

principal

recede

ruthless

sacrifice

Improve each of the following sentences by crossing out the bold phrase and replacing it with a word (or a form of the word) from Word List 9.

1. Oil is the **most important** export of Saudi Arabia.

2. John Hancock wrote his name with a **decorative sweeping line** when he signed the Declaration of Independence.

3. In Greek myths, an animal was sometimes **slaughtered as an offering** by a mortal to please the gods.

4. Some people believe you have to be **unwilling to show any pity to those with whom you have dealings** in order to succeed in business.

5. Many childhood memories **gradually become fainter and fainter** as we grow older.

6. Tennis suffered a **serious and very sad** loss when Arthur Ashe died.

7. The **period in history given the name** of "the cold war" ended in 1990 with the easing of tension between the United States and the Soviet Union.

8. If this heavy rain continues, soil erosion will **follow as a result of it.**

9. The **soldiers housed in a protected place** suffered few casualties during the attack.

Circle the letter or letters of each correct answer. A question may have more than one correct answer.

1. Which of the following responses might **placate** an irate customer?
   (a) "Don't blame me; I just work here."
   (b) "I'll take care of the problem."
   (c) "Would you calm down!"
   (d) "Let me get the manager."

2. A town can be **inundated** with which of the following?
   (a) floodwaters
   (b) tourists
   (c) winds of hurricane force
   (d) requests for tourist information

3. Which of the following can **flourish?**
   (a) a business
   (b) a country
   (c) a tree
   (d) an incident

4. Which of the following could be the length of an **era?**
   (a) one year
   (b) twenty seconds
   (c) a couple of centuries
   (d) a couple of hours

5. Which of the following can be **hoarded?**
   (a) health
   (b) wealth
   (c) food
   (d) solitude

6. Which of the following is true of a **nomad?**
   (a) is part of a group
   (b) has a permanent home
   (c) works at a 9 to 5 job
   (d) lives mostly in cities

7. Which of the following applies to the word **principal?**
   (a) It is not a noun.
   (b) It can be a noun or an adjective.
   (c) It is a noun only.
   (d) It is an adjective only.

8. Which of the following can be **grievous?**
   (a) a wound
   (b) a respite
   (c) a loss
   (d) a privilege

dumbfound

ensue

era

flourish

garrison

grievous

hoard

inundate

invincible

nomad

placate

principal

recede

ruthless

sacrifice

Write a synonym for each of the numbered words. Choose from the boldfaced words below.

consider	**joy**	**amaze**	**satisfy**	**hasty**
manage	**overcrowded**	**brave**	**proud**	**beg**

1. cope _____

2. congested _____

3. beseech _____

4. ponder _____

5. gratify _____

6. haughty _____

7. dumbfound _____

8. rapture _____

9. impetuous _____

10. plucky _____

9E ▷ Passage

Read the passage. Then answer the questions that follow it.

The Spanish Conquest of Mexico

For over two hundred years, until it was overthrown by Spanish invaders in 1519, the Aztec empire in Mexico was a prosperous and highly cultivated society. Many arts and sciences **flourished;** the Aztecs developed astronomy, mathematics, engineering, agriculture, sculpture, and music to a far higher degree than did the Europeans of that **era.** At the same time, they were a warlike people, **ruthless** in battle, and their religious beliefs involved acts of extreme cruelty. Prisoners of war were offered as human **sacrifices** to their many gods. The Aztecs believed that the gods had already destroyed the world four times, and unless they were **placated** in this way, they would destroy it again.

The Aztecs were originally a **nomadic** people who lived mainly by hunting. Around the year 1300, they settled on an island on Lake Texcoco. The land there was wet and swampy, but the Aztecs drained the marshes and became farmers. Their **principal** crop was corn; they also grew beans, squash, and chili peppers. Over a two-hundred-year period, they created an empire extending across central Mexico from the Gulf of Mexico to the Pacific. Its capital was Tenochtitlán, which we know today as Mexico City. In 1500, Tenochtitlán was **inundated** by a terrible flood that drowned many of its people. After the floodwaters had **receded,** the Aztecs quickly rebuilt their city, but a far worse catastrophe was to follow.

In 1519, a Spanish explorer named Hernando Cortéz landed in Mexico with an army of 600 soldiers. He established a **garrison** in what is now the city of Veracruz on Mexico's east coast. His plan was to destroy the Aztec army and take over their country for Spain. Because horses were unknown to the Aztecs, they were **dumbfounded** by the sight of people on horseback. They believed the Spanish soldiers to be gods and therefore **invincible.** Fighting them, the Aztecs thought, would be pointless. So Montezuma, the Aztec emperor, allowed the Spaniards to take over his city without any resistance. Cortéz now gave the orders and Montezuma became a prisoner in his own palace. The Spanish discovered a great **hoard** of gold and silver there. It was later loaded onto Spanish ships and sent to Spain. It is believed that much of the treasure was lost at sea.

dumbfound

ensue

era

flourish

garrison

grievous

hoard

inundate

invincible

nomad

placate

principal

recede

ruthless

sacrifice

When word came that Spanish soldiers had been killed in an attack on Veracruz, the Aztecs realized that they had made a **grievous** error in their previous thinking. These strange creatures were not gods after all! A battle **ensued** in Tenochtitlán, and although Montezuma was killed, the Aztecs drove the Spanish from their city. But their victory was only temporary. Cortéz returned in 1521 with another army that laid siege to Tenochtitlán. After eighty days, the city was forced to surrender. The rule of the Aztecs in Mexico had ended; Spanish rule had begun.

▶ **Answer each of the following questions in the form of a sentence. If a question does not contain a vocabulary word from the lesson's word list, use one in your answer. Use each word only once.**

1. When did the Aztecs give up their **nomadic** way of life?

_____

_____

2. What is the meaning of **flourished** as it is used in the passage?

_____

_____

3. What is the meaning of **principal** as it is used in the passage?

_____

_____

4. Why would thieves find Montezuma's palace especially appealing?

_____

_____

5. What **grievous** event occurred in Tenochtitlán in 1500?

_____

_____

6. Why would neighboring tribes not want to antagonize the Aztecs?

_____

_____

7. What was an initial part of Cortéz's plan to conquer Mexico?

_____

_____

8. What shocked the Aztecs when they first saw the Spaniards?

_____

_____

9. How do we know that the Aztecs feared their gods?

_____

_____

10. What is the meaning of **sacrifices** as it is used in the passage?

_____

_____

11. Why did the Aztecs capitulate so readily?

_____

_____

12. What **ensued** after the second surrender of Tenochtitlán?

_____

_____

13. In what year did the Aztec **era** end?

_____

_____

14. What is the meaning of **receded** as it is used in the passage?

_____

_____

15. What is the meaning of **inundated** as it is used in the passage?

_____

_____

dumbfound

ensue

era

flourish

garrison

grievous

hoard

inundate

invincible

nomad

placate

principal

recede

ruthless

sacrifice

- **Flourish** and *flower* (as verbs) are synonyms; both can mean "to thrive." We can say that the arts *flourished*, or *flowered*, in Athens in the fifth century B.C.E. Both words come from the Latin *flos*, which means "a flower."

- Don't confuse **hoard**, "something stored away secretly," with *horde*, "a large crowd or swarm." These two words are homophones; they sound the same but have different spellings and meanings.

- Don't confuse **principal** with *principle*, which has three meanings: (1) "a rule or truth by which we govern ourselves" (The *principle* of the separation of church and state traces to the First Amendment); (2) "a truth from which other truths can be worked out" (One *principle* of plane geometry is that parallel lines never meet); (3) "a rule or law that explains how something works" (An electric bell works on the *principle* of the continuous making and breaking of an electric current).

Lesson 10

Word List	Study the definitions of the words. Then do the exercises that follow.

aquatic
ə kwät´ ik

adj. 1. Growing or living in or on water.
Water lilies are **aquatic** plants.

2. Done in or upon water.
Water skiing is an **aquatic** sport.

assert
ə sʉrt´

v. To say firmly; to declare.
Charles **asserted** that the money entrusted to him was in a safe place.

assertion *n.* A firm statement or declaration.
No one challenged her **assertion** that Tuckerman's Ravine was too dangerous to ski.

assertive *adj.* Self-assured; bold and confident.
Because of his **assertive** manner, he was able to obtain an interview for the job.

avert
ə vʉrt´

v. 1. To turn away.
I **averted** my eyes from the scary scenes in the movie.

2. To keep from happening.
The driver **averted** an accident by hitting the brake.

bleak
blēk

adj. 1. Without much hope.
The company's future looked **bleak** when the new product failed to sell.

2. Cold and dreary; exposed to cold winds and bad weather.
Penguins seem to flourish in Antarctica's **bleak** climate.

blithe
blīth

adj. 1. Cheerful; carefree.
The children's **blithe** mood is captured beautifully in the Renoir painting.

2. Not showing proper care; heedless.
The driver showed a **blithe** indifference for the safety of others on the highway.

blithely *adv.* In a carefree manner.
I was reminded of her highly positive attitude when she walked **blithely** out the door.

docile
däs´ əl

adj. Well behaved; easy to handle.
Because it was my first attempt at riding, I was given the most **docile** horse in the stable.

dwindle dwin´dəl	*v.* To keep on becoming less; to grow smaller in number or amount. My hopes of winning the arm wrestling match **dwindled** when I saw the size of my opponent's muscles.
lethal lē´thəl	*adj.* Causing, or capable of causing, death. A rattlesnake's bite can be **lethal.**
monitor män´i tər	*v.* To watch closely and frequently; to observe and make note. Some cities **monitor** the amount of pollution in the air. *n.* A video screen used to display information. The sales clerk checked the **monitor** to see if the book was still in stock.
mutilate myo͞ot´l āt	*v.* To hurt or damage by cutting into, cutting off, or cutting out. Steel traps are cruel because they **mutilate** the animals caught in them.
nimble nim´bəl	*adj.* 1. Able to move quickly and easily. Karen's **nimble** fingers plucked the harp strings with amazing speed. 2. Showing quickness of thinking; clever. It takes a **nimble** mind to solve such a difficult problem.
plight plīt	*n.* A difficult or dangerous condition or situation. The **plight** of homeless people was the principal subject of tonight's evening news.
ponderous pän´dər əs	*adj.* Heavy and slow moving. The elephant made its way with **ponderous** steps through the clearing.
verge vʉrj	*n.* An edge, border, or brink. After being on the **verge** of extinction, the bald eagle made a remarkable comeback in the 1980s. *v.* To come close to the edge or border of. The story is not merely silly; it **verges** on the ridiculous.
vigilant vij´ə lənt	*adj.* Watchful; ready for danger. Health authorities remain **vigilant** for any signs of the epidemic's return.

Choose two phrases to form a sentence that correctly uses a word from Word List 10. Write each sentence in the space provided.

1. (a) be the cause of it.
   (b) To mutilate something is to
   (c) To avert something is to
   (d) prevent it from happening.

   _____

   _____

2. (a) To monitor something is to
   (b) hide it from view.
   (c) To assert something is to
   (d) declare it forcefully.

   _____

   _____

3. (a) To mutilate something is to
   (b) cause it to happen.
   (c) To verge on something is to
   (d) hurt it by cutting into it.

   _____

   _____

4. (a) A blithe response is one
   (b) that is meant to intimidate.
   (c) that shows quickness of mind.
   (d) A nimble response is one

   _____

   _____

5. (a) A vigilant creature is one
   (b) whose bite can cause death.
   (c) that is watchful.
   (d) A docile creature is one

   _____

   _____

6. (a) A plight is
   (b) A monitor is
   (c) a video screen that displays information.
   (d) a blatant denial of what is clearly true.

   _____

   _____

7. (a) can be changed as needed.
   (b) suggests no future problems.
   (c) A blithe response is one that
   (d) A bleak response is one that

   _____

   _____

8. (a) a difficult situation.
   (b) A verge is
   (c) an amusing diversion.
   (d) A plight is

   _____

   _____

aquatic
assert
avert
bleak
blithe
docile
dwindle
lethal
monitor
mutilate
nimble
plight
ponderous
verge
vigilant

9. (a) A fortune that verges   (c) A fortune that dwindles
   (b) increases monthly.   (d) decreases in size.

_____

_____

10B ▷ **Just the Right Word**

Improve each of the following sentences by crossing out the bold phrase and replacing it with a word (or a form of the word) from Word List 10.

1. Ramone **said in a very forceful way** that a ten-year-old is competent to babysit.

2. You have to be **able to move quickly and easily** to get on the gymnastics team.

3. Household chemicals such as bleach and other cleaning products can be **capable of causing death** if swallowed.

4. This machine **keeps a check on** the patient's condition around the clock.

5. The White Mountains can be very **cold and dreary with strong winds and bad weather** in winter.

6. Some plants are **of a kind that flourish in water,** so they do not need soil in order to grow.

7. Such negligence in maintaining the vehicle **comes close to bordering** on indifference to the passengers' safety.

8. Although its bark is intimidating, the dog is actually quite **easy to control.**

9. Following the accident, the driver drove off **as though not caring,** seemingly unaware of the damage to his car.

10. Walruses are **heavy and slow moving** on land but graceful in the water.

11. I **turned away** my eyes from the light when it became too bright.

Circle the letter or letters of each correct answer. A question may have more than one correct answer.

1. Which of the following are **aquatic** activities?
   - (a) boating
   - (b) scuba diving
   - (c) golfing
   - (d) sunbathing

2. Which of the following is **ponderous?**
   - (a) a mouse
   - (b) a planet
   - (c) a bulldozer
   - (d) a hippopotamus

3. Which of the following can be **nimble?**
   - (a) a mind
   - (b) a tree
   - (c) a squirrel
   - (d) a dancer

4. Which of the following might be a **plight?**
   - (a) being evicted
   - (b) inheriting money
   - (c) being a casualty
   - (d) facing a ruthless opponent

5. Which of the following might an **assertive** person say?
   - (a) "Get in line."
   - (b) "You don't belong here!"
   - (c) "I was here first."
   - (d) "Oh no, you don't!"

6. Which of the following can be **bleak?**
   - (a) a region
   - (b) a mountain
   - (c) a statement
   - (d) a delicacy

7. Which of the following can be **lethal?**
   - (a) a snake bite
   - (b) a gunshot wound
   - (c) a garland
   - (d) a reprimand

8. Which of the following might a **docile** person do?
   - (a) push to the front of the line
   - (b) wait patiently until called
   - (c) get irate with a sales clerk
   - (d) admonish a stranger

aquatic
assert
avert
bleak
blithe
docile
dwindle
lethal
monitor
mutilate
nimble
plight
ponderous
verge
vigilant

Write an antonym for each of the numbered words. Choose from the boldfaced words below.

| kind | fierce | miserable | advance | lax |
| ponderous | annoy | hopeful | harmless | increase |

1. placate _____

2. recede _____

3. lethal _____

4. ruthless _____

5. dwindle _____

6. docile _____

7. blithe _____

8. nimble _____

9. vigilant _____

10. bleak _____

Read the passage. Then answer the questions that follow it.

Danger: Manatees at Play

The subject of manatees takes us far back in the history of both natural science and imaginative storytelling. Manatees have been in existence for fifty million years. This sea animal was probably what sailors were seeing long ago when they reported visions of mermaids sunning themselves on rocks far in the distance.

Closer observation of the manatee shows it to be a **ponderous** mammal. It measures from eight to twelve feet in length and weighs up to 3,000 pounds. The manatee's tapered body, shaped somewhat like that of an overgrown seal or miniature whale, has two front legs and a broad flat tail. The legs and the tail all act as flippers.

Manatees live singly or in small groups. They can eat 200 pounds of food a day, grazing contentedly on water hyacinths and other **aquatic** plants. A manatee sometimes may stand up straight in the water, often with strings of sea plants hanging like hair from its head.

In the United States, Florida's coastal waters are the manatee's principal habitat. These sea creatures are quite **docile** by nature. In fact, they have no fear of humans; they seem to love company! Manatees allow swimmers to play alongside them, something that is discouraged by game wardens.

Florida authorities **monitor** the manatee population carefully. A 2009 aerial survey showed that more than 2,000 manatees inhabit the area's waters. Manatees were once hunted for their hides and their meat. However, they have been protected by law from this practice for more than a century. Still, the alarming reality is that the manatee population has **dwindled** considerably in recent years. Sadly, this lovable creature, which has survived all these years without threats from predators, may now be on the **verge** of extinction. The main reason for this is related to the enormous increase in the number of powerboats in Florida.

Manatees feed just below the surface. They are often unobserved by speeding boaters who may go **blithely** on their way, ignorant of the terrible injuries they have just inflicted. Being struck by a high-speed propeller can be **lethal;** almost a third of all manatee deaths are boat-related, and the number is growing. Wildlife wardens estimate that ninety percent of all adult manatees have been **mutilated** by the propellers of speeding boats. The reasons for

aquatic
assert
avert
bleak
blithe
docile
dwindle
lethal
monitor
mutilate
nimble
plight
ponderous
verge
vigilant

this are not entirely clear—perhaps the manatees have poor hearing and are unaware of a boat's approach. Perhaps they are simply not **nimble** enough to get out of the way in time.

In recent years, people have become more aware of the **plight** of the manatee. Laws such as the Endangered Species Act and the Marine Mammal Protection Act prohibit harming manatees. More needs to be done, though. People operating power boats in areas where manatees live need to be more **vigilant.** If they were, many collisions could be **averted.** And speed limits need to be strictly enforced, even though people whose livelihood depends on the boating industry **assert** that too much regulation would cause economic hardship. One thing is certain: if speedboats continue to operate as they have in the past, the ancient manatee's prospects of survival are **bleak.**

▶ **Answer each of the following questions in the form of a sentence. If a question does not contain a vocabulary word from the lesson's word list, use one in your answer. Use each word only once.**

1. What behavior of manatees could have made sailors mistakenly **assert** that they had seen a mermaid?

_____

_____

2. What kind of plant is a water hyacinth?

_____

_____

3. Is the nature of the manatee similar to that of a predator?

_____

_____

4. Is the manatee population increasing or decreasing?

_____

_____

5. Have many manatees have been injured as a result of collisions with boats?

_____

_____

6. Can a manatee die as a result of being struck by the propeller of a boat?

_____

_____

7. Why do many boaters go **blithely** on their way after striking a manatee?

_____

_____

8. What could boat owners do to protect the manatee population?

_____

_____

9. What is the meaning of **averted** as it is used in the passage?

_____

_____

10. How do we keep track of the manatee population?

_____

_____

11. Why would manatees be described as **ponderous?**

_____

_____

12. What is the meaning of **nimble** as it is used in the passage?

_____

_____

13. Why should we be concerned about the manatee?

_____

_____

14. What is the meaning of **bleak** as it is used in the passage?

_____

_____

15. Are people indifferent to the manatees' **plight?**

_____

_____

aquatic
assert
avert
bleak
blithe
docile
dwindle
lethal
monitor
mutilate
nimble
plight
ponderous
verge
vigilant

- The Latin word for *water* is *aqua* and forms the root of the adjective **aquatic.** Other words formed from this root include nouns such as *aquarium* and *aqueduct,* "a large pipe or channel for water." You might guess that the word *aquiline* comes from the same Latin root. Actually, it comes from a different Latin word altogether, *aquila,* which means "eagle." An *aquiline* nose is one that is curved like an eagle's beak.

- The ancient Greeks believed that the dead went to the underworld, where they bathed in the river Lethe, which caused them to forget their earthly lives. The Latin word *letum,* "death," comes from the name of the river and forms the English adjective **lethal,** "capable of causing death" (a *lethal* injection; a *lethal* weapon).

- The noun **plight** carries with it a reminder of love and marriage in centuries past. Once it was a verb and meant "to promise; to pledge." When persons got engaged to be married, they "plighted their troth." This means they would dishonor themselves if they were not faithful and true to each other. *Troth* is a word that has disappeared entirely from the language. Once it meant "loyalty; faithfulness; honor."

- Several words come from the Latin *vigilare,* "to be watchful." In addition to **vigilant,** there is *vigil,* a watch kept during normal hours of sleep (Parents keep a *vigil* by the bedside of a very sick child) and *vigilante,* a person who takes the law into her or his own hands, usually as part of a group.

For more practice and games, go to **www.WordlyWise3000.com**.

Word List	Study the definitions of the words. Then do the exercises that follow.

ballast
bal´ əst

n. Heavy material used to make a ship steady or control the rising and falling of a vessel like a balloon.
The hot air balloon rose when the water used as **ballast** was let go.

buoyant
boi´ ənt

adj. 1. Able to float.
The life jackets are **buoyant** enough to support a 200-pound person.

2. Cheerful and carefree.
The students were in a **buoyant** mood on the last day of school.

buoyancy *n.* The ability to float.
The **buoyancy** of helium balloons causes them to rise rapidly.

clamber
klam´ bər

v. To climb awkwardly.
I **clambered** onto the roof to get the kite.

detach
dē tach´

v. To separate from.
I **detached** the upper portion of the bill and returned it with my payment.

detached *adj.* 1. Not connected.
The house comes with a **detached** garage.

2. Lacking concern; not taking sides.
I tried to stay **detached** from my friends' quarrel.

eerie
ir´ ē

adj. Causing uneasiness; strange or mysterious.
The **eerie** sound you heard was just an owl hooting.

fathom
fath´ əm

n. A length of six feet, used in measuring the depth of water.
The wreck of the Spanish ship lay in thirty **fathoms** of water.

v. To figure out; to understand.
We could not **fathom** how the magician made the goldfish disappear.

pique
pēk

v. To arouse or excite.
Pandora's curiosity was **piqued** by the mysterious box that she was not supposed to open.

n. A feeling of resentment caused by being ignored, insulted, etc.
It was the scientist's **pique** at not being invited to take part in the experiment that caused him to write that derogatory article about it.

probe
prōb

v. 1. To poke or prod.
I **probed** the snow with my ski pole to determine how deep it was.

2. To examine closely.
The *Odyssey* space craft was launched in 2001 to **probe** the surface of the planet Mars.

n. 1. A long, slender instrument used to examine a wound or part of the body.
The doctor used a **probe** to look for fragments of glass in the wound.

2. A thorough investigation.
The police **probe** into illegal gambling led to twelve arrests.

realize
rē´ ə līz

v. 1. To be aware of.
I didn't **realize** how astute you were until you came up with that brilliant idea.

2. To bring into being; to make happen.
I **realized** a lifelong dream by going skydiving.

rupture
rup´ chər

v. To split or break.
Frost **ruptured** the water pipe, flooding the basement.

n. 1. A breaking or tearing apart by force.
The earthquake caused a **rupture** in the highway that took three months to repair.

2. The breaking of a friendly relationship.
The **rupture** between Cuba and the United States began when Fidel Castro seized control of the island.

sphere
sfir

n. 1. An object with all points on its surface equally distant from its center; a ball or globe.
The earth is not quite a **sphere** because it is flattened at the poles.

2. An area of power, influence, or activity.
The 1823 Monroe Doctrine extended the United States' **sphere** of influence throughout the Americas.

spherical   *adj.* Of or relating to the shape of a sphere.
The **spherical** lamp threw light in all directions.

submerge
sub mʉrj´

v. 1. To go underwater.
From the shore, we could see the dolphins jump and then **submerge.**

2. To put underwater or cover with water.
The tide **submerges** the rocks when it is high.

tedious
tē´ dē əs

adj. Seeming to go on for a long time; boring.
The lecture was so **tedious** that I nearly fell asleep.

tedium   *n.* Boredom.
We tried to relieve the **tedium** of our long drive by telling jokes.

ultimate ul´tə mət	*adj.* 1. Final. Anwar's **ultimate** goal is to be chief of surgery at a teaching hospital. 2. The greatest possible; maximum. The producer has **ultimate** control over the movie. *n.* Something that is the greatest; the maximum. The ads claim that this soap is the **ultimate** in cleaning products.
unscathed un skāthd´	*adj.* Completely unharmed. Because of its sturdy construction, the house survived the hurricane **unscathed.**

11A Finding Meanings

Choose two phrases to form a sentence that correctly uses a word from Word List 11. Write each sentence in the space provided.

1. (a) be baffled by it.
   (b) To realize a dream is to
   (c) make it happen.
   (d) To fathom a dream is to

_____

_____

2. (a) material used to make a ship steady.
   (b) a feeling of gloom.
   (c) Buoyancy is
   (d) Ballast is

_____

_____

3. (a) A sphere is
   (b) a measurement of depth.
   (c) A fathom is
   (d) something forgotten.

_____

_____

4. (a) To probe a person's interest
   (b) is to satisfy it.
   (c) is to arouse it.
   (d) To pique a person's interest

_____

_____

5. (a) A sphere is
   (b) A rupture is
   (c) a breaking apart by force.
   (d) an inquiry into the cause of something.

_____

_____

ballast
buoyant
clamber
detach
eerie
fathom
pique
probe
realize
rupture
sphere
submerge
tedious
ultimate
unscathed

6. (a) it is separated from the rest.   (c) If something is eerie,
   (b) If something is detached,   (d) it is added to something else.

   _____

   _____

7. (a) a feeling of resentment.   (c) Buoyancy is
   (b) Pique is   (d) fear of the unknown.

   _____

   _____

8. (a) is to be unharmed.   (c) is to show a lack of interest.
   (b) To be tedious   (d) To be unscathed

   _____

   _____

9. (a) To clamber is to   (c) To probe is to
   (b) remove oneself.   (d) examine closely.

   _____

   _____

10. (a) An ultimate task is one that   (c) is impossible to do.
    (b) is very boring.   (d) A tedious task is one that

   _____

   _____

Improve each of the following sentences by crossing out the bold phrase and replacing it with a word (or a form of the word) from Word List 11.

1. The **unnatural and strange** silence that filled the deserted house was suddenly shattered.

2. The police could not **figure out exactly** how the painting had been stolen from the museum.

3. When I moved to Alaska, I didn't **have any idea** how much I would miss my friends.

4. This damaged life jacket may have lost some of its **ability to keep a person afloat.**

5. The college president will head the **thorough inquiry** into the causes of student unrest.

6. I've ridden many roller coasters, but the Corkscrew Cannonball is without any doubt the **one that is greater than all the rest.**

7. While I was telling her my troubles, my friend seemed curiously **uninvolved in what I was saying.**

8. Nuclear submarines can **go underwater** for several weeks.

9. I **climbed with difficulty** over the rocks to get to the sea wall.

10. A banker by profession, she was also involved in politics, diplomacy, and other **areas of activity.**

ballast
buoyant
clamber
detach
eerie
fathom
pique
probe
realize
rupture
sphere
submerge
tedious
ultimate
unscathed

Circle the letter or letters of each correct answer. A question may have more than one correct answer.

1. Which of the following would make a good **ballast?**
   (a) iron bars
   (b) helium gas
   (c) sand
   (d) straw

2. Which of the following could be **fathomed?**
   (a) a purpose
   (b) a puzzle
   (c) a motive
   (d) a mystery

3. For which of the following might a **probe** be used?
   (a) brain surgery
   (b) a soccer game
   (c) a picnic
   (d) a flat tire

4. Which of the following can be **submerged?**
   (a) waves
   (b) the sun
   (c) a submarine
   (d) an anchor

5. Which of the following can be **buoyant?**
   (a) a person's spirits
   (b) a life jacket
   (c) an anchor
   (d) a brick

6. Which of the following might **rupture?**
   (a) a friendship
   (b) a balloon
   (c) a gas tank
   (d) an epidemic

7. Which of the following is **spherical?**
   (a) a pingpong ball
   (b) a hockey puck
   (c) a rainbow
   (d) a ball bearing

8. Which of the following can one **detach?**
   (a) the ink from a pen
   (b) the toothpaste from the tube
   (c) a postage stamp from a roll
   (d) a page from a notebook

Complete the analogies by selecting the pair of words whose relationship most resembles the relationship of the pair in capital letters. Circle the letter of the pair you choose.

1. CIRCLE : SPHERE ::
   (a) link : chain
   (b) length : breadth
   (c) triangle : rectangle
   (d) square : cube

2. FATHOM : DEPTH ::
   (a) ocean : water
   (b) ounce : weight
   (c) mystery : understanding
   (d) inch : foot

3. TEDIOUS : EXCITEMENT ::
   (a) ruthless : mercy
   (b) irate : anger
   (c) dumbfounded : surprise
   (d) warm : heat

4. STRINGS : PLUCK ::
   (a) clothes : wear
   (b) drum : beat
   (c) candle : glow
   (d) water : flow

5. DELECTABLE : DELICIOUS ::
   (a) melodious : music
   (b) dilapidated : building
   (c) generous : benefactor
   (d) derogatory : insulting

6. FLOWER : GARLAND ::
   (a) soil : garden
   (b) actor : agent
   (c) seed : plant
   (d) link : chain

7. FLOAT : BUOYANT ::
   (a) juggle : nimble
   (b) sink : aquatic
   (c) flourish : active
   (d) probe : eerie

8. HOARD : HORDE ::
   (a) peek : pique
   (b) burn : fire
   (c) lend : bend
   (d) slice : knife

9. AQUATIC : WATER ::
   (a) delicate : delicacy
   (b) solar : sun
   (c) full : moon
   (d) spherical : earth

10. SMOLDER : BLAZE ::
    (a) dampen : submerge
    (b) clamber : awkward
    (c) deny : assert
    (d) avoid : avert

ballast

buoyant

clamber

detach

eerie

fathom

pique

probe

realize

rupture

sphere

submerge

tedious

ultimate

unscathed

Read the passage. Then answer the questions that follow it.

Exploring Earth's Last Frontier

By the middle of the twentieth century, the earth's continents had been explored from pole to pole. But even though water covers three-quarters of the earth's surface, much of the deep ocean floor remained a mystery. Auguste Piccard, a Belgian scientist whose curiosity was **piqued** by the unknown, changed that. In 1932, he had broken the world's altitude record by going ten miles up in a balloon. He next planned to design and build a vessel to explore the deepest parts of the ocean.

On October 26, 1948, Piccard made his first dive off the coast of Africa in a bathyscaphe, a large, hollow, **spherical** vessel made of thick steel. The word comes from two Greek words: *bathys,* "deep," and *scaphe,* "a light boat." The bathyscaphe could descend into the inky blackness of the ocean depths. With its powerful searchlights, it could **probe** the ocean floor. Those inside were able to look out through windows made of thick layers of acrylic plastic. **Buoyancy** was provided by huge tanks containing gasoline, which is lighter than seawater. The vessel hung beneath these tanks. Iron weights fixed to the outside of the hull by magnets were used as **ballast,** causing the bathyscaphe to descend.

The first test dive was made in water where the seabed lay just twelve **fathoms** below the surface. Piccard and the other crew member were bolted inside the bathyscaphe, which was then swung over the side of the support ship and **submerged.** As the vessel sank below the surface, it filled with an **eerie** blue light, created by sunlight passing through the water. It took just a few minutes for the two pioneers of underwater exploration to reach the ocean floor. Shortly afterward, Piccard **detached** the iron weights; the bathyscaphe rose to the surface.

Several hours passed while the gasoline tanks were emptied; this had to be completed before the two men were able to **clamber** out of their cramped quarters. Despite the **tedious** wait, Piccard was a happy man. His mind was already on his **ultimate** dream, to explore the very deepest part of the ocean. He was asked later if he had been afraid during the descent. He replied that he had total confidence in the design and the construction of the vessel he had invented; and, therefore, he had no reason to be afraid.

Twelve years later, Piccard's son Jacques **realized** his father's dream. He and a United States naval officer descended seven miles in a newer, larger, and stronger bathyscaphe to explore the deepest part of the Pacific Ocean. They knew that if there were a single defect in the metal, the enormous pressure would cause cracks to develop. That would **rupture** the vessel and crush them both. There was no way for them to escape if anything went wrong. Thankfully, the two crew members emerged **unscathed** after their great adventure. Jacques Piccard's father, who at the age of seventy-six was considered too old to make the descent himself, was waiting on the recovery vessel and was the first to greet them.

▶ **Answer each of the following questions in the form of a sentence. If a question does not contain a vocabulary word from the lesson's word list, use one in your answer. Use each word only once.**

1. What is the meaning of **probe** as it is used in the passage?

_____

_____

2. Did the bathyscaphe stay underwater long on its first dive?

_____

_____

3. What caused the bathyscaphe to sink to the bottom of the sea?

_____

_____

4. Why did Piccard **detach** the iron weights?

_____

_____

5. What strange experience did the men in the first bathyscaphe have as they dived?

_____

_____

ballast

buoyant

clamber

detach

eerie

fathom

pique

probe

realize

rupture

sphere

submerge

tedious

ultimate

unscathed

6. Why was it necessary to empty the gasoline from the tanks after Auguste Piccard's dive?

_____

_____

7. What is the depth of water that is equal to 72 feet?

_____

_____

8. How would you describe the period of time between Auguste Piccard's arrival at the surface and his emergence from the vessel?

_____

_____

9. Why was it vital that the hull of Jacques Piccard's vessel have no defects?

_____

_____

10. What is the meaning of **realized** as it is used in the passage?

_____

_____

11. What was the condition of the two men who exited their bathyscaphe after exploring the deepest part of the Pacific Ocean?

_____

_____

12. In what way did Piccard's son Jacques resemble his father?

_____

_____

13. What is the meaning of **ultimate** as it is used in the passage?

_____

_____

14. Why would the bathyscaphe have looked the same from any direction?

_____

_____

15. Why were the large tanks filled with gasoline?

_____

_____

FUN & FASCINATING FACTS

- The fact that the same word can be used as a unit of measurement and as a synonym for _understand_ might at first seem strange. With the word **fathom,** however, the connection is easy to see. Sailors wanting to know the depth of the water would drop a weighted line, marked off in fathoms, or six-foot lengths, over the side of the boat. When the weight reached the bottom, the length of line indicated how deep the sea was at that point. Sailors would say that they had "fathomed" its depth. By extension, a person who was able to "get to the bottom of" something unknown or puzzling was said to have _fathomed_ the mystery.

The word itself has an interesting history; it comes from the Old English _faethm,_ the distance from fingertip to fingertip of a tall person's outstretched arms. In many cases, this is about six feet.

- The word **sphere** comes from the Greek word for a ball, which is _sphaira._ By combining _sphere_ with the Greek word _hemi_ ("half"), we get _hemisphere,_ which is _half_ of a _sphere._ Earth is divided into a northern _hemisphere_ (everywhere north of the equator) and a southern _hemisphere_ (everywhere south of the equator). Earth can also be divided into an eastern _hemisphere_ and a western _hemisphere._

ballast

buoyant

clamber

detach

eerie

fathom

pique

probe

realize

rupture

sphere

submerge

tedious

ultimate

unscathed

For more practice and games, go to www.WordlyWise3000.com.

Word List

Study the definitions of the words. Then do the exercises that follow.

abduct
ab dukt´

v. To carry away by force; to kidnap.
Bandits stopped the jeep and **abducted** the driver.

abduction   *n.* The act or instance of abducting.
According to Greek myth, the **abduction** of Helen was the cause of the Trojan War.

abode
ə bōd´

n. The place where one lives; home.
My summer **abode** was a small cabin that I shared with two other camp counselors.

abyss
ə bis´

n. 1. A deep opening in the earth.
We were afraid to look down as we crossed the **abyss** on a swaying rope bridge.

2. Anything too deep to measure.
The Hubble space telescope was built to probe the **abyss** of space.

arbitrate
är´ bi trāt

v. To settle a disagreement between two parties by having a third party make a decision after hearing both sides.
The United Nations will **arbitrate** the border dispute between the two countries.

arbitration   *n.* (ar bi trā´ shən) The act of arbitrating.
By agreeing to **arbitration,** management and workers hope to avoid a strike.

attribute
ə trib´ yōot

v. To think of as coming from or belonging to a particular person or thing.
The painting was wrongly **attributed** to Mary Cassatt, America's foremost Impressionist artist.

n. (a´ tri byōot) A quality or feature associated with a person or thing.
Wisdom is often considered an **attribute** of old age.

capricious
kə prish´ əs

adj. Likely to change quickly for no obvious reason.
Robert Frost wrote an amusing poem about the **capricious** New England weather.

compromise
käm´ prə mīz

v. 1. To settle a disagreement by having each side give up something.
We **compromised** by splitting the difference between the $2,000 asking price of the car and the $1,500 offer I made for it.

2. To expose to the possibility of criticism or shame.
The manager will not **compromise** the restaurant's reputation by tolerating poor service to diners.

n. A settlement reached by each side giving up something.
The **compromise** required me to work late on Fridays so that I could have Saturdays off.

devout
də vout´

adj. 1. Very religious.
Devout Muslims try to make at least one visit to the holy city of Mecca.

2. Sincere.
I am a **devout** believer in the healing power of the mind.

distraught
di strôt´

adj. Deeply disturbed; very troubled.
The children were **distraught** when their pet rabbit died.

enlighten
en līt´ n

v. To inform or instruct; to give knowledge or truth to.
Since we didn't know the store's policy for returning merchandise, we asked customer service to **enlighten** us.

enlightened *adj.* Free from ignorance or prejudice.
This day-care center takes an **enlightened** approach to early childhood education.

incline
in klīn´

v. 1. To slope or lean.
Instead of being vertical, the post **inclines** slightly to the left.

2. To be likely to; to have a fondness for.
I am **inclined** to talk too much.

3. To bend or bow (the head).
I **inclined** my head so that the barber could trim the back of my neck.

n. (in´ klīn) A sloping surface.
The summer house lay at the top of a grassy **incline.**

intervene
in tər vēn´

v. To enter in order to help or settle something.
The playground supervisor **intervened** when the children couldn't agree about whose turn it was.

intervention *n.* (in tər vən´ shən) The act or instance of intervening.
The talk show host's timely **intervention** kept the discussion from becoming too heated.

necessity
nə ses´ ə tē

n. 1. Anything that cannot be done without or that is greatly needed.
Insect repellent is a **necessity** when camping.

2. The condition of being needed.
I don't see the **necessity** for taking separate cars.

| **orbit** | *n.* The path taken by an object around a heavenly body such as a star, planet, or moon. |
| ôr´ bit | |

The moon's **orbit** around the earth takes just over 27 days.

v. To put into or be in orbit.
In 1961, the Russian Yuri Gagarin became the first human being to **orbit** the earth.

| **sacred** | *adj.* 1. Holy; having to do with religion. |
| sā´ krəd | |

The Western Wall in Jerusalem is **sacred** to the Jewish people.

2. Worthy of being given the greatest honor or respect.
The engaged couple asserted that they consider marriage vows to be **sacred.**

12A ▷ Finding Meanings

Choose two phrases to form a sentence that correctly uses a word from Word List 12. Write each sentence in the space provided.

1. (a) a bowing of the head.   (c) An attribute is
   (b) a quality associated with a person.   (d) A compromise is

   _____

   _____

2. (a) A necessity is   (c) a sloping surface.
   (b) a sudden change of mind.   (d) An incline is

   _____

   _____

3. (a) expose to criticism.   (c) To abduct is to
   (b) To compromise is to   (d) keep from danger.

   _____

   _____

4. (a) An abyss is   (c) the path taken by an object around a heavenly body.

   (b) An orbit is   (d) the distance of a planet from the sun.

   _____

   _____

5. (a) one who acts suddenly on a whim.
   (b) one who is deeply disturbed.
   (c) A distraught person is
   (d) A devout person is

   _____

   _____

6. (a) A capricious promise is one
   (b) made unwillingly.
   (c) made with great seriousness.
   (d) A sacred promise is one

   _____

   _____

7. (a) To enlighten someone is to
   (b) offer protection to that person.
   (c) To abduct someone is to
   (d) carry off that person by force.

   _____

   _____

8. (a) anything that is considered necessary.
   (b) anything that is too deep to measure.
   (c) An abyss is
   (d) An abode is

   _____

   _____

9. (a) the condition of being needed.
   (b) a promise to pay.
   (c) Arbitration is
   (d) Necessity is

   _____

   _____

10. (a) To be enlightened about something
    (b) To intervene in something
    (c) is to avoid it completely.
    (d) is to involve oneself in it.

    _____

    _____

11. (a) To be inclined to something is
    (b) To arbitrate something is
    (c) to find a use for it.
    (d) to have a fondness for it.

    _____

    _____

abduct

abode

abyss

arbitrate

attribute

capricious

compromise

devout

distraught

enlighten

incline

intervene

necessity

orbit

sacred

Improve each of the following sentences by crossing out the bold phrase and replacing it with a word (or a form of the word) from Word List 12.

1. In order to prevent a strike, the union members decided to **settle for less than they had hoped for,** and so they accepted a smaller pay increase.

2. Nimbleness is one of the **qualities that is typical** of Olympic gymnasts.

3. Each morning, the chanting of the **very religious** worshippers drifted from the temple.

4. He greeted them by saying, "Welcome to my new **residence, the place that I call home."**

5. The space shuttle **travels in a path around** Earth every ninety minutes.

6. It's difficult to maintain a close friendship with someone who is so **quick to change from one moment to the next for no obvious reason.**

7. The two sides decided to settle their dispute through **the process in which a third party helps settle the matter.**

8. Television should **provide information to** viewers as well as entertain them.

9. I **slightly bent** my body toward the speaker in order to hear what she was saying.

Circle the letter or letters of each correct answer. A question may have more than one correct answer.

1. Which of the following can be **arbitrated?**
   (a) quarrels
   (b) nomads
   (c) differences
   (d) casualties

2. Which of the following can be **capricious?**
   (a) an action
   (b) a sphere
   (c) the weather
   (d) a garden

3. Which of the following might be considered a **compromise?**
   (a) settling for less
   (b) demanding more
   (c) antagonizing the other party
   (d) accepting an impartial judgment

4. Which of the following can be **sacred?**
   (a) places
   (b) books
   (c) whims
   (d) objects

5. Which of the following are **necessities?**
   (a) food
   (b) shelter
   (c) decorations
   (d) entertainment

6. Which of the following can **enlighten** people?
   (a) books
   (b) radio
   (c) movies
   (d) speeches

7. Which of the following can be an **abode?**
   (a) a hovel
   (b) a palace
   (c) a bicycle
   (d) a boat

8. Which of the following travel in **orbit?**
   (a) Earth
   (b) a river
   (c) Venus
   (d) the moon

abduct
abode
abyss
arbitrate
attribute
capricious
compromise
devout
distraught
enlighten
incline
intervene
necessity
orbit
sacred

Change each of the words below into a different part of speech by adding, removing, or changing a suffix. Write the new word on the line. All words are from this lesson or previous lessons.

Verb	Adjective
1. disrupt	_____
2. gratify	_____
3. dumbfound	_____
4. assert	_____
5. detach	_____

Noun	Adjective
6. pluck	_____
7. nomad	_____
8. sphere	_____
9. privilege	_____
10. congestion	_____

Verb	Noun
11. disrupt	_____
12. aspire	_____
13. enroll	_____
14. impede	_____
15. intimidate	_____

Read the passage. Then answer the questions that follow it.

How the Seasons Changed

We know that the seasons occur because the earth, as it travels in its yearly **orbit** around the sun, has its northern hemisphere tilted away from the sun during northern winters and toward it during northern summers. The ancient Greeks were less **enlightened** in matters of astronomy than we are today. They had a different explanation. It was expressed in one of their myths about the goddess Demeter and her daughter Persephone.

The ancient Greeks believed that the gods **intervened** frequently in human affairs and often did so in a **capricious** manner. They were **inclined** to look upon mortals as mere playthings. Demeter, whose name means "earth mother," was different. She was a benevolent goddess who had given humans the gift of agriculture, which provided them with most of the **necessities** of life. The island of Sicily was especially **sacred** to the ancient Greeks. They believed it was there that Demeter had first given corn to humans. Women, who tilled the fields and planted the crops while the men hunted, were among her most **devout** followers.

According to the myth, Persephone was **abducted** by Hades, the god of the underworld, while she was in a field with her friends picking flowers. He suddenly rose from an **abyss** that he created at her feet. He then carried Persephone off to his home, the **abode** of the dead. There he made her his wife. **Distraught** over the loss of her daughter, Demeter searched for her everywhere. When at last she discovered what had happened, Demeter demanded that Persephone be returned to her. Hades refused. He argued that Persephone had eaten a pomegranate while in the underworld. Anyone who had taken food there could never leave.

Unable to agree on a solution to the problem, Demeter and Hades called upon Zeus, the ruler of the gods, to **arbitrate** the dispute. Demeter threatened to make the earth barren unless her daughter was restored to her. Zeus did not want to lose the humans who worshipped him. So he worked out a **compromise.** Persephone would live part of each year in the underworld with Hades. The rest of the year she would spend on earth with her mother.

And so, we see, it is to Demeter's moods that the ancient Greeks **attributed** the changing of the seasons. During the summer months, when

abduct

abode

abyss

arbitrate

attribute

capricious

compromise

devout

distraught

enlighten

incline

intervene

necessity

orbit

sacred

the land in Greece is scorched by the hot southern sun and crops wither in the heat, Persephone was thought to be in the underworld with Hades. During the mild, moist months from fall to spring when the earth is fruitful, she was living on earth with her mother.

▶ **Answer each of the following questions in the form of a sentence. If a question does not contain a vocabulary word from the lesson's word list, use one in your answer. Use each word only once.**

1. Were the ancient Greek gods remote from human affairs?

_____

_____

2. Why was it difficult to predict how the gods might behave?

_____

_____

3. What do we know to be the cause of the change of seasons?

_____

_____

4. What is the meaning of **inclined** as it is used in the passage?

_____

_____

5. Was Demeter indifferent to the loss of her daughter?

_____

_____

6. Did Persephone go willingly with Hades to the underworld?

_____

_____

7. Why was Zeus's **arbitration** of the dispute successful?

_____

_____

8. What is the meaning of **abyss** as it is used in the passage?

_____

_____

9. What is the meaning of **compromise** as it is used in the passage?

_____

_____

10. Why would the Greeks have built many temples on the island of Sicily?

_____

_____

11. Why would the ancient Greeks have worshipped Demeter?

_____

_____

12. Why must the region ruled by Hades have been a very gloomy place?

_____

_____

13. Why do we understand the change of seasons better than the ancient Greeks did?

_____

_____

14. Does Earth go around the sun or does the sun go around Earth?

_____

_____

15. What are some of the **necessities** of life?

_____

_____

abduct
abode
abyss
arbitrate
attribute
capricious
compromise
devout
distraught
enlighten
incline
intervene
necessity
orbit
sacred

- **Abyss** comes from the Greek *bussos,* which means "bottom," combined with the prefix *a-,* which means "without." The adjective formed from it is *abysmal,* which means "too deep or too great to be measured." Because this adjective is often used to modify negative qualities (*abysmal* ignorance, *abysmal* poverty), it has acquired a secondary meaning, "very bad" or "wretched." (The choir's *abysmal* performance was the result of inadequate preparation.)

- The adjective **distraught** is formed from the Latin verb *trahere,* "to draw" or "pull," combined with the prefix *dis-,* "apart." To be *distraught* is to be so agitated or upset that one's attention is likely to be drawn away from or pulled apart from whatever might otherwise engage it. The verb *distract* is formed in the same way. To be *distracted* is to have one's attention drawn away from whatever ought to engage it. (The band playing in the street outside *distracted* me from my studies.) A person who is *distraught* experiences strong emotion; this is not necessarily the case with a person who is *distracted.*

Hidden Message   In the boxes provided, write the words from Lessons 9 through 12 that are missing in each of the sentences. The number following each sentence gives the word list from which the missing word is taken. When the exercise is finished, the shaded boxes should spell out a haiku by the Japanese poet Nozawa Boncho. A haiku is a poem of three lines and seventeen syllables, with a subject often taken from nature. This haiku is called "Winter."

1. A thousand-foot-deep _____ blocked our way. **(12)**

2. The _____ of the Roman Empire ended in 410 C.E. **(9)**

3. The giant strode with _____ steps across the stage. **(10)**

4. A _____ in the gas line caused the explosion. **(11)**

5. Her _____ attitude cheered up her co-workers. **(10)**

6. No serious person would _____ that the earth is flat. **(10)**

7. The Koran is a _____ book to Muslims. **(12)**

8. The _____ of the homeless children broke our hearts. **(10)**

9. I am a _____ believer in the value of exercise. **(12)**

10. A telephone is really a _____ in the modern world. **(12)**

11. Neither side in the dispute was willing to _____. **(12)**

12. Sit down, because what I have to say will _____ you. **(9)**

13. The dog looks fierce but is actually quite _____. **(10)**

14. The spaceship went into _____ around the earth at noon. **(12)**

15. A _____ person will often act on a whim. **(12)**

16. You need to be pretty _____ to play in the outfield. **(10)**

17. I was so _____ by the news that I forgot to call. **(12)**

18. Minnesota winters can be pretty _____. **(10)**

19. Stuffing envelopes all day is _____ work. **(11)**

20. The ball rolled gently down the _____. **(12)**

21. A _____ sailor happened to see the raft floating by. **(10)**

22. Tell this joke and laughter will _____. **(9)**

23. This machine will _____ your pulse and breathing. **(10)**

24. Count Dracula's _____ was a castle in Transylvania. **(12)**

25. I _____ my success to good luck and hard work. **(12)**

26. These plants will _____ if given plenty of sunshine. **(9)**

27. Your quick action helped to _____ an accident. **(10)**

28. She is trying to reduce the _____ on her mortgage. **(9)**

29. We had to _____ over the rocks to get to the beach. **(11)**

30. The _____ prize in the Olympics is a gold medal. **(11)**

31. Listeners _____ KROC radio with their requests. **(9)**

32. Here's a news item that will _____ your interest. **(11)**

33. In 1972, *Pioneer 10* was sent to _____ beyond the solar system. **(11)**

34. By 1945, Hitler's once _____ army was in ruins. **(9)**

35. The cutters can _____ your hand if the guard is left off. **(10)**

36. These ancient and much-feared warriors were _____ in battle. **(9)**

37. The death of my grandfather was a _____ loss to us all. **(9)**

38. I cannot _____ his motive for leaving so abruptly. (11)

39. A retired judge has agreed to _____ the dispute. (12)

40. This vessel can _____ and stay underwater for days. (11)

41. At the time, I did not _____ how much I owed you. (11)

42. The kidnappers used a trick to _____ the government official. (12)

43. Someone who fears hunger may _____ food. (9)

44. A young goat was killed as a _____ to the gods. (9)

45. A billiard or pool ball should be a perfect _____. (11)

46. A _____ moves with the herds in search of fresh pastures. (9)

47. Our unexpected victory put us in a _____ mood. (11)

48. We tried to avoid having our savings _____ away. (10)

For more practice and games, go to **www.WordlyWise3000.com**.

Word List	Study the definitions of the words. Then do the exercises that follow.

arduous
är´ jōō əs

adj. Requiring much effort; very difficult.
Frequent sandstorms made the **arduous** trek across the Sahara Desert even more difficult.

canny
kan´ ē

adj. Shrewd and careful; watchful of one's own interests.
A **canny** businessperson can make a profit even in the worst of times.

climax
klī´ maks

n. The highest point; the greatest moment or event.
Slugger Norris's winning home run in the World Series was a terrific **climax** to the season.

endorse
en dôrs´

v. 1. To sign the back of a check before cashing or depositing it.
The bank teller wouldn't cash my check until I had **endorsed** it.

2. To approve of; to support.
Newspapers often **endorse** candidates for public office.

3. To be favorably associated with a product in return for payment.
Some well-known athletes are paid millions of dollars to **endorse** products on television.

exuberant
eg zōō´ bər ənt

adj. Happy and excited; bubbling over with enthusiasm.
Our friends gave us an **exuberant** welcome at the airport.

exuberance *n.* The quality of being exuberant.
The steady rain could not dampen the **exuberance** of fans gathered for the rock festival.

intrepid
in trep´ id

adj. Feeling or showing no fear; brave; courageous.
The **intrepid** astronauts brought their crippled *Apollo 13* spacecraft safely back to Earth.

kindle
kin´ dəl

v. 1. To start burning.
A spark from the wood stove **kindled** some oily rags and started the fire.

2. To cause to become excited or stirred up.
The museum's exhibition of Navaho pottery **kindled** my interest in the Southwest.

kindling *n.* (kind´ liŋ) Sticks used to start a fire.
There were plenty of dry twigs to provide **kindling** for the campfire.

lucrative lōō′ krə tiv	*adj.* Producing wealth or profit. I invested some of the money I had inherited in what sounded like a **lucrative** deal.
mentor men′ tər	*n.* A wise and loyal friend and adviser. As president of the college she founded, Mary McLeod Bethune was a **mentor** to many young black women.
obsession äb sesh′ ən	*n.* An interest, idea, or feeling that fills one's mind and leaves little room for anything else. Finishing her second novel has become an **obsession** with her and leaves her little time for other activities.
personable pʉr′ sən ə bəl	*adj.* Pleasing in manner and appearance. The hotel's **personable** staff made our stay a pleasant one.
proficient prō fish′ ənt	*adj.* Able to do something very well; skillful. All the mechanics in this garage are **proficient** in car repairing. **proficiency** *n.* The quality of being proficient. My cousin's **proficiency** in Japanese enabled her to make many friends in Tokyo.
scanty skan′ tē	*adj.* Not enough or just barely enough; small in size or amount. After a **scanty** meal of a bread roll and an apple, we continued our journey.
strait strāt	*n.* A narrow body of water connecting two larger ones. The **Strait** of Gibraltar connects the Mediterranean Sea and the Atlantic Ocean. **straits** *n.* Trouble or need. When both parents lost their jobs, the family was in desperate **straits.**
zest zest	*n.* Great enjoyment; excitement. Learning to scuba dive added **zest** to our Caribbean vacation. **zestful** *adj.* Full of zest. During the second week of my new exercise program, I awoke each day feeling **zestful** and ready for a five-mile run.

Choose two phrases to form a sentence that correctly uses a word from Word List 13. Write each sentence in the space provided.

1. (a) A strait is
   (b) a fear without a known cause.
   (c) an idea that takes over one's mind.
   (d) An obsession is

   _____

   _____

2. (a) An exuberant person
   (b) is one who is brave.
   (c) A canny person
   (d) is one who seldom makes mistakes.

   _____

   _____

3. (a) one that is difficult.
   (b) An arduous task is
   (c) A lucrative task is
   (d) one that is done without payment.

   _____

   _____

4. (a) to make it work.
   (b) To kindle something is
   (c) To endorse something is
   (d) to sign the back of it.

   _____

   _____

5. (a) a narrow channel of water.
   (b) A strait is
   (c) a narrow ledge of rock.
   (d) A climax is

   _____

   _____

6. (a) wood used to start a fire.
   (b) Zest is
   (c) Kindling is
   (d) support for a person or a cause.

   _____

   _____

7. (a) A climax is
   (b) A mentor is
   (c) a person who is vulnerable.
   (d) a wise teacher.

   _____

   _____

8. (a) keen enjoyment.
   (b) Proficiency is
   (c) Zest is
   (d) the absence of fear.

   _____

   _____

9. (a) in short supply.
   (b) seriously defective.
   (c) If something is lucrative, it is
   (d) If something is scanty, it is

   _____

   _____

10. (a) Exuberance is
    (b) Proficiency is
    (c) a state of great need.
    (d) a state of excitement.

    _____

    _____

13B ▶ Just the Right Word

Improve each of the following sentences by crossing out the bold phrase and replacing it with a word (or a form of the word) from Word List 13.

1. Getting a telescope **got me excited and stirred up** my interest in astronomy.

2. In this course, students must demonstrate **that they have reached a certain level of skill** in both drawing and painting.

3. Firefighters need to be **unafraid of physical danger** but cannot take foolish risks.

4. This year's citrus crop will be **much smaller than usual** because of the frost damage in Florida.

5. The **greatest event** of Navratilova's career was her ninth Wimbledon singles victory in 1990.

6. My mother is a **trusted friend and wise adviser** to several young ballerinas.

7. Terry's part-time baked-goods business turned out to be quite **rewarding in a financial way.**

8. The new television announcer is extremely **pleasing both in manner and appearance.**

arduous
canny
climax
endorse
exuberant
intrepid
kindle
lucrative
mentor
obsession
personable
proficient
scanty
strait
zest

9. What **narrow body of water** is it that separates Spain from North Africa?

10. Will the students' parents **give their support to** the controversial proposal?

13c ▶ Applying Meanings

Circle the letter or letters of each correct answer. A question may have more than one correct answer.

1. Which of the following might describe someone who is **personable?**
   (a) ruthless
   (b) amiable
   (c) astute
   (d) haughty

2. Which of the following can reach a **climax?**
   (a) a game
   (b) a novel
   (c) a painting
   (d) a movie

3. Which of the following could be **endorsed?**
   (a) a candidate
   (b) a check
   (c) athletic equipment
   (d) a proposal

4. Which of the following can be **kindled?**
   (a) firewood
   (b) enthusiasm
   (c) curiosity
   (d) negligence

5. Which of the following might be a good **mentor?**
   (a) an illustrious person
   (b) a devious person
   (c) a person devoid of good sense
   (d) a candid person

6. Which of the following would show a **zest** for learning?
   (a) reading books
   (b) asking questions
   (c) watching cartoons
   (d) dropping out of school

7. Which of the following can be **exuberant?**
   (a) a reprimand
   (b) a welcome
   (c) a person
   (d) a compromise

8. Which of the following might become someone's **obsession?**
   (a) indifference
   (b) another person
   (c) food
   (d) exercise

Synonyms have the same or almost the same meanings, but one often fits a sentence better. Choose the word that best fits each sentence.

arduous / difficult

1. Japanese is a(n) _____ language to learn.

2. The trek across the Gobi Desert was a(n) _____ journey.

religous / devout

3. The Koran is a _____ text that is the basis of Islam.

4. A _____ Muslim prays five times a day.

intrepid / brave

5. The _____ astronauts brought *Apollo 13* safely back to Earth.

6. Josie tries to be _____ when she goes to the dentist.

instruct / enlighten

7. A good teacher seeks to _____ her students.

8. Please _____ the mail carrier to leave any packages for me.

clamber / climb

9. We train the rosebushes to _____ the trellis.

10. I saw the boys run away and _____ up the wall.

final / ultimate

11. Malcolm's go-cart entered the _____ lap.

12. Scientists disagree about the _____ fate of the rain forests.

abode / home

13. Mount Olympus was the Greek gods' _____ .

14. George Washington's _____ was called Mount Vernon.

hopeless / bleak

15. Only penguins can survive the _____ Antarctic winter.

16. Feeling _____ , the candidate dropped out of the race.

arduous
canny
climax
endorse
exuberant
intrepid
kindle
lucrative
mentor
obsession
personable
proficient
scanty
strait
zest

stringent/strict

17. Grandma tells us that she had a very _____ upbringing.

18. The product testers performed a series of _____ tests.

surrender/capitulate

19. The police ordered the thief to _____ .

20. The mayor did not _____ to the demand for lower taxes.

13E   Passage

Read the passage. Then answer the questions that follow it.

America's First Lady of the Sky

In 1917, Amelia Earhart was working as a nurse's helper in Canada, caring for pilots wounded in the First World War. Their stories **kindled** an interest in flying in the nineteen-year-old girl, and so after the war she took lessons and became a **proficient** pilot. As soon as she had saved enough money, she bought her own plane. She soon broke the women's altitude record, taking her tiny biplane up to 14,000 feet. By that time, flying had become an **obsession.** Earhart's **zest** for adventure led her to become the first woman to fly solo across the Atlantic. She also became the first person to make the perilous solo flight from Hawaii to California. Previous attempts had claimed the lives of ten pilots.

In 1931, she married publisher George Putnam. A **canny** businessperson, Putnam acted as his wife's manager and was her **mentor** in the ways of business. In addition to being world famous for her exploits in the air, Earhart was **personable** and enjoyed being in the spotlight. This made it easy for Putnam to promote her activities. He published the books she wrote. He got her contracts with advertisers to **endorse** products. He also set up **lucrative** speaking tours in which Earhart talked not only about flying but also about other issues important to her, such as women's rights and world peace. The money they earned in these ways was used to help meet the high costs of buying and maintaining Earhart's aircraft.

On June 1, 1937, at the age of thirty-nine, Earhart took off in a twin-engine Lockheed Electra on a round-the-world flight. Accomplishing this long-term goal was to be the **climax** of her career. The event, which began by heading east from California, attracted worldwide interest. **Exuberant** crowds greeted her at every stop of the flight, eager to catch a glimpse of the **intrepid** flier. On the morning of July 2, she took off on the most **arduous** leg of the journey, a 2,500-mile flight from New Guinea to tiny Howland Island in the middle of the Pacific Ocean. Twenty hours into the flight, having covered most of the journey, Earhart radioed that she was running out of fuel. She never made it to Howland Island. Massive air and sea rescue missions produced no clues as to her fate.

Amelia Earhart's disappearance remained a complete mystery for over fifty years. Then, in 1992, searchers found part of a shoe that may have belonged to Earhart together with some scraps of aluminum, possibly from her plane, on Nikumaroro Island, 500 miles south of Howland Island. The plane could have crash-landed there when it ran out of fuel. If this is indeed what happened, Earhart and her navigator would have been in desperate **straits.** They could not have survived more than a few days. Temperatures on the island reach 120 degrees. They would have had only a **scanty** supply of water on board, and there was none on the island. Their bodies, and the remains of the plane, would have been swept out to sea in a relatively short time. Is this what actually happened to Amelia Earhart? It is a likely explanation, but we will probably never know for sure.

▶ **Answer each of the following questions in the form of a sentence. If a question does not contain a vocabulary word from the lesson's word list, use one in your answer. Use each word only once.**

1. Why would Earhart have been successful as a television personality?

_____

_____

2. What led Earhart to buy her own plane?

_____

_____

3. How might her flying instructor have rated Earhart?

_____

_____

arduous
canny
climax
endorse
exuberant
intrepid
kindle
lucrative
mentor
obsession
personable
proficient
scanty
strait
zest

4. What is the meaning of **endorse** as it is used in the passage?

_____

_____

5. What qualification did George Putnam have to manage Earhart's career?

_____

_____

6. How did the various deals that Putnam set up help Earhart?

_____

_____

7. What two important roles did Putnam play in Earhart's life?

_____

_____

8. What is the meaning of **kindled** as it is used in the passage?

_____

_____

9. Why must Earhart have felt **exuberant** when she flew solo across the Atlantic?

_____

_____

10. Why was the 1937 round-the-world flight so important to Earhart?

_____

_____

11. Why did the flight from New Guinea to Howland Island require special care?

_____

_____

12. What would have made thirst a particular problem for the stranded fliers?

_____

_____

13. What is the meaning of **straits** as it is used in the passage?

_____

_____

14. What led Earhart to engage in her dangerous exploits?

_____

_____

15. Why would *timid* not be an appropriate word to describe Earhart?

_____

_____

FUN & FASCINATING FACTS

- The adjective formed from the word **climax** is *climactic*. (The *climactic* scene in a movie is the one toward which the earlier scenes have been leading.) Don't confuse this word with *climatic*, which is the adjective form of *climate*. (The great ice ages were the result of *climatic* changes.)

- The Latin *dorsum* means "back" and occurs in several English words. The *dorsal* fin of a fish is the one growing from its back; the familiar triangular fin of a shark is perhaps the best-known example. Our word **endorse** comes from this same Latin root. When you *endorse* a check or other document, you sign your name on the back of it.

- A **mentor** is a wise friend and counselor, one who takes responsibility for another person's education and instructs her or him in the ways of business or a profession. The word comes from Homer's great epic poem *The Odyssey*. While its main character Odysseus was engaged in his adventurous travels, his friend Mentor was entrusted with the running of his household and with the education of his son Telemachus.

arduous

canny

climax

endorse

exuberant

intrepid

kindle

lucrative

mentor

obsession

personable

proficient

scanty

strait

zest

For more practice and games, go to **www.WordlyWise3000.com.**

Word List	Study the definitions of the words. Then do the exercises that follow.

allege
ə lej´

v. To state as a fact but without offering proof.
The police **allege** that the two teenagers took the car without permission.

alleged *adj.* Claimed to be true.
This is the **alleged** troublemaker.

allegation *n.* (al ə gā´ shən) Something that is alleged.
Our neighbor claimed that my brother was the boy who broke his window, but he could not provide proof to back up his **allegation.**

conclusive
kən klōō´ siv

adj. Putting an end to doubt; convincing.
The cancelled check was **conclusive** proof that the bicycle had been paid for.

counterpart
koun´ tər pärt

n. A person or thing that is similar to another.
The British prime minister is the **counterpart** of the American president.

dismal
diz´ məl

adj. 1. Dark or extremely gloomy.
The **dismal** weather kept us inside for most of our vacation at the beach.

2. Causing misery or sadness; depressing.
The **dismal** conditions in Haiti forced many to flee their homeland.

enthrall
en thrôl´

v. To hold the attention of as though under a spell.
The acrobats on the trapeze **enthralled** the circus audience.

enthralling *adj.* Having the power to enthrall.
The children listened for over an hour to the storyteller's **enthralling** tales.

exotic
eg zät´ ik

adj. Fascinating because of being very different from the ordinary.
Rare orchids and other **exotic** flowers decorated the tables at the wedding.

incredulous
in krej´ ə ləs

adj. 1. Doubtful; skeptical.
The teacher was **incredulous** when the student claimed to have read the novel in two hours.

2. Showing disbelief.
My friend gave me an **incredulous** look when I said I had seen a flying saucer.

incredulity *n.* (in krə dyōō´ lə tē) Doubt or disbelief.
My father gave me a look of **incredulity** when I said I had asked for extra homework.

legendary lej´ ən der ē	*adj.* 1. Well-known; famous and much talked about over a long period of time. Harriet Tubman, who led more than 300 slaves to freedom, is a **legendary** figure in American history. 2. Relating to a story (usually untrue) handed down from the past. Paul Bunyan, the **legendary** lumberjack of fantastic size and strength, is the hero of many "tall tales."
lurk lʉrk	*v.* To prowl or lie hidden, as though about to attack. The farmer frightened away the fox that **lurked** by the henhouse.
menagerie mə naj´ ər ē	*n.* A collection of animals kept in cages for showing to the public. The owner of the **menagerie** assured us that the animals were well cared for.
naive nä ēv´	*adj.* 1. Inexperienced; ready to accept without analyzing. I was **naive** to believe that sending off the coupon would win me a free vacation in Hawaii. 2. Simple in a childlike way; innocent. Even though he is nine years old, he maintains a **naive** belief in the tooth fairy.
pander pan´ dər	*v.* To give or promise what is wanted in order to please someone. I believe that she **panders** to students by giving them better grades than they deserve.
plausible plô´ zə bəl	*adj.* Seeming to be true but not necessarily so. Lin Shao's explanation of why she was late seems **plausible,** so I'll accept it.
preposterous prē päs´ tər əs	*adj.* Too absurd to be believed; ridiculous. You cannot believe this **preposterous** newspaper story that a six-month-old baby speaks three languages.
scrupulous skrōō´ pyə ləs	*adj.* 1. Marked by close attention to the smallest detail. The treasurer kept a **scrupulous** record of all moneys received and paid out. 2. Acting in a correct and honest manner. The children were **scrupulous** in the way they divided the money from the lemonade stand.

Choose two phrases to form a sentence that correctly uses a word from Word List 14. Write each sentence in the space provided.

1. (a) An incredulous person is someone
   (b) who is not telling the truth.
   (c) who has a childlike innocence.
   (d) A naive person is someone

   _____

   _____

2. (a) A counterpart is
   (b) a collection of animals.
   (c) a plant with healing properties.
   (d) A menagerie is

   _____

   _____

3. (a) To lurk is to
   (b) To pander is to
   (c) be prepared to defend oneself.
   (d) hide so as to attack without warning.

   _____

   _____

4. (a) A dismal story
   (b) is one that is believable.
   (c) A plausible story
   (d) is one made up as one goes along.

   _____

   _____

5. (a) Allegations are things that have
   (b) Counterparts are things that have
   (c) much in common with each other.
   (d) nothing to do with each other.

   _____

   _____

6. (a) An enthralling story is one
   (b) A dismal account is one
   (c) that is depressing.
   (d) that is quite unbelievable.

   _____

   _____

7. (a) A preposterous offer is
   (b) one that is made in writing.
   (c) An alleged offer is
   (d) one that cannot be taken seriously.

   _____

   _____

8. (a) is careful to avoid wrongdoing.
   (b) A legendary person is one who
   (c) is careless of others' feelings.
   (d) A scrupulous person is one who

   _____

   _____

9. (a) one that can be taken two ways.   (c) one that expresses disbelief.
   (b) An incredulous reply is   (d) A conclusive reply is

_____

_____

14B ▷ Just the Right Word

Improve each of the following sentences by crossing out the bold phrase and replacing it with a word (or a form of the word) from Word List 14.

1. We loved Tahiti, the tropical paradise in the South Pacific, because it was so **fascinatingly different and so far away.**

2. The squirrel didn't see the cat **waiting to attack while hiding** in the bushes.

3. We think we know what caused the gas pipe to rupture, but the evidence is not **strong enough to put an end to all doubt.**

4. There is no **other planet that is in any way similar** to Earth.

5. Her **statement that is not backed by proof** is that someone entered the house while she was away.

6. Robin Hood is a **famous character in stories handed down from the past but is probably not a real** figure.

7. The small children were **so attentive that they seemed to be under a spell cast** by Barney, the television dinosaur.

8. It's not a good idea for parents to **try to provide satisfaction by giving in** to their child's every whim.

9. When I first heard their story about finding a wallet full of money, I was **unable to accept it as true.**

10. To say that I would lie to protect myself is **too absurd to be believed.**

11. When you believed the promises in the chain letter, you were being **very foolish because of your inexperience in these matters.**

allege
conclusive
counterpart
dismal
enthrall
exotic
incredulous
legendary
lurk
menagerie
naive
pander
plausible
preposterous
scrupulous

Circle the letter or letters of each correct answer. A question may have more than one correct answer.

1. Which of the following could be **plausible?**
   (a) an offer
   (b) a solution
   (c) an excuse
   (d) a lie

2. Which of the following expresses **incredulity?**
   (a) "That's impossible!"
   (b) "You're pulling my leg."
   (c) "Is that so?"
   (d) "I suppose it's possible."

3. Which of the following could be **enthralling?**
   (a) a movie's climax
   (b) a tedious story
   (c) an indifferent performance
   (d) strenuous toil

4. Which of the following might be found in a **menagerie?**
   (a) tigers
   (b) wolves
   (c) kittens
   (d) whales

5. Which of the following is an **exotic** first name?
   (a) Jane
   (b) Whoopee
   (c) Moonbeam
   (d) Jack

6. Which of the following could be **dismal?**
   (a) the weather
   (b) a forecast
   (c) a weekend
   (d) a hovel

7. Which of the following is a **legendary** figure?
   (a) Babe Ruth
   (b) Billy the Kid
   (c) Sandra Day O'Connor
   (d) Cleopatra

8. Which of the following could be **scrupulous?**
   (a) a person
   (b) an inspection
   (c) an incident
   (d) a privilege

The prefix *in-* means "not" and usually changes a word into its opposite. But not all words beginning with *in* contain this prefix. Study the words and decide which ones begin with the prefix *in-* meaning "not." If the word does contain the prefix *in-*, write *yes*. If it does not, write *no*.

1. incident   _____

2. inefficient   _____

3. incline   _____

4. incredulous   _____

5. indifferent   _____

6. industrious   _____

7. inconspicuous _____

8. intervene   _____

9. incompetent   _____

10. inevitable   _____

11. inundate   _____

12. infuriate   _____

13. inadequate   _____

14. inherit   _____

15. inconclusive   _____

16. initiate   _____

17. inconvenient _____

18. intensify   _____

19. intimidate   _____

20. intrepid   _____

allege

conclusive

counterpart

dismal

enthrall

exotic

incredulous

legendary

lurk

menagerie

naive

pander

plausible

preposterous

scrupulous

Read the passage. Then answer the questions that follow it.

Bigfoot: Fact or Fantasy?

When European explorers returned from Asia and Africa in the Middle Ages, they reported having seen twelve-foot lizards with huge jaws that could eat a person whole. Most people who heard these stories were **incredulous** and accused the travelers of lying. The stories seemed **preposterous** to them. At that time hardly anyone in Europe had ever seen a crocodile. For centuries, travelers have been ridiculed for their reports of **exotic** creatures seen in distant lands. But the Komodo dragon of Indonesia, the giant panda of Western China, and the mountain gorilla of Ethiopia, to mention just three that were dismissed at one time as imaginary, really do exist.

More recently, there have been stories of Bigfoot, the **legendary** ape-like creature of the American Northwest. And Bigfoot's **counterpart** is said to live just below the snowline in the Himalayan Mountains of Asia. It is the yeti, also known as the Abominable Snowman. **Alleged** sightings, and even photographs, of both creatures make news periodically. Plaster casts have supposedly been made of their footprints. But the photographs are never sharp; the plaster casts could well be fakes; and the claims of those who say they have seen Bigfoot are not very **plausible.** Scientists have been **scrupulous** in their examination of the evidence. Their view is that it is not **conclusive.** Most remain unconvinced that Bigfoot and the yeti actually exist.

In spite of the scientists' findings, some people feel the need to believe that such creatures do exist. Such people are **enthralled** by the mysterious. They would like to think that somewhere deep in the forest, Bigfoot is **lurking.** They imagine that high in the Himalayas, a team of mountaineers is about to come upon the yeti. Supermarket tabloids **pander** to these people. They print headlines such as "Bigfoot Stole My Baby" or "Yeti Attacks Climbers on Mount Everest." Of course, only the most **naive** people believe such stories.

Given our **dismal** record of dealing with wild creatures, it would probably be best for Bigfoot and the yeti, if indeed they *are* real, to remain undiscovered. What would we do with them if we captured them? Such creatures do not belong in a **menagerie** to be peered at and photographed by sightseers. Such is the fate of the giant panda, the Komodo dragon, and the mountain gorilla. Bigfoot and the yeti are probably best left where they are now, creatures of our imagination, along with unicorns, fire-breathing dragons, and mermaids.

▶ **Answer each of the following questions in the form of a sentence. If a question does not contain a vocabulary word from the lesson's word list, use one in your answer. Use each word only once.**

1. Do tabloid newspapers do a responsible job of reporting the news?

_____

_____

2. What is the meaning of **naive** as it is used in the passage?

_____

_____

3. What do Bigfoot and the Abominable Snowman have in common?

_____

_____

4. How does the yeti compare with Bigfoot?

_____

_____

5. What do many people imagine Bigfoot to be doing?

_____

_____

6. Where would a creature like Bigfoot *not* belong?

_____

_____

7. What is the meaning of **incredulous** as it is used in the passage?

_____

_____

8. What is the meaning of **scrupulous** as it is used in the passage?

_____

_____

allege
conclusive
counterpart
dismal
enthrall
exotic
incredulous
legendary
lurk
menagerie
naive
pander
plausible
preposterous
scrupulous

9. Why does the passage describe spottings of Bigfoot as "**alleged**"?

_____

_____

10. Why do most people not accept claims of Bigfoot sightings?

_____

_____

11. What kind of evidence would lead scientists to believe that Bigfoot exists?

_____

_____

12. What would be a likely reaction of people should there be a more convincing account of a Bigfoot sighting?

_____

_____

13. What is the meaning of **dismal** as it is used in the passage?

_____

_____

14. Why would a rabbit not be considered an **exotic** creature?

_____

_____

15. Why would a report that a unicorn had been spotted be **preposterous?**

_____

_____

- The adjective **dismal** is formed from two Latin words: *dies,* "day," and *mal,* "bad." It is easy to see how having a bad day might make a person feel dismal.

- The Old English word *thrael* means "a slave" and survives in our modern English word **enthrall,** one of whose meanings is "to enslave." The more common meaning, "to hold as if in a spell," can suggest a kind of enslavement; to be enthralled by someone is to be so fascinated by him or her that one surrenders one's will to that person.

- The Latin verb *credere* means "to believe" and is used in the formation of a number of English words. *Credulous* persons are easily fooled because they are inclined to believe whatever they are told, no matter how unlikely. On the other hand, persons who are **incredulous** find it hard to believe what they are being told. A *credible* story is one that sounds believable. An *incredible* story is one that is hard to believe.

- A *scruple* is a twinge or sense of guilt felt when one wants to do something that one shouldn't. A **scrupulous** person is someone who has scruples and won't do something that is wrong or dishonest. Some people have no scruples and will do whatever is necessary to further their own purposes. They are *unscrupulous.*

allege

conclusive

counterpart

dismal

enthrall

exotic

incredulous

legendary

lurk

menagerie

naive

pander

plausible

preposterous

scrupulous

For more practice and games, go to **www.WordlyWise3000.com**.

| **Word List** | Study the definitions of the words. Then do the exercises that follow. |

complement
käm´ plə mənt

n. 1. Something that completes or makes perfect.
Candles will be the perfect **complement** for an elegant dinner.

2. The number or amount that makes up a whole.
The shelf has a full **complement** of books.

v. To bring to completion or perfection.
These CDs of Joan Baez in concert will **complement** my collection of folk music.

component
kəm pō´ nənt

n. Any of the more important parts of a whole.
The picture tube is the main **component** of a television set.

adj. Contributing to form a whole.
A tape deck and a CD player are two of the **component** parts of a complete stereo system.

conjure
kän´ jər

v. 1. To call forth by magic, or as if by magic.
Shakespeare's Hotspur claims that he can **conjure** spirits.

2. (with *up*) To bring to mind; to recall or evoke.
The aroma of baking bread **conjures** up memories of my childhood.

emphasize
em´ fə sīz

v. To give special attention to; to stress.
The teacher **emphasized** that homework must be turned in on time.

emphasis   *n.* (em´ fə sis) Special attention directed at something to give it importance.
The course covers the period 1845–1860 with **emphasis** on the causes of the Civil War.

emphatic   *adj.* (em fat´ ik) Said or done with force.
When asked when she planned to retire, her answer was an **emphatic** "Never!"

homage
häm´ ij

n. Honor or respect shown publicly.
On Veteran's Day, we pay **homage** to those who gave their lives for their country.

impromptu
im prämp´ tōō

adj. Unplanned.
She gave a charming **impromptu** speech when called upon by the host.

adv. Without preparation.
This speech course teaches students to speak **impromptu.**

lush
lush

adj. Marked by richness of growth, especially of vegetation.
Arid volcanic terrain contrasts sharply with **lush** mountains on the island's opposite side.

medley
med´ lē

n. 1. A mixture of often unrelated things.
On the yard sale's bargain table was a **medley** of objects priced at under a dollar.

2. A selection of music from various sources, played as one piece.
The concert ended with a **medley** of patriotic tunes.

oblige
ə blīj´

v. 1. To require someone to do something for legal, social, or moral reasons.
Joining the book club **obliges** you to buy four selections over the year.

2. To earn the gratitude of.
You will **oblige** me by saying no more about this matter.

3. To do a favor for.
We begged Miss Streisand to **oblige** us with one final song.

pretentious
prē ten´ shəs

adj. Drawing undeserved or inappropriate attention to oneself; showy.
Was it **pretentious** of John Hancock to sign his name so conspicuously to the Declaration of Independence?

prowess
prou´ əs

n. Great skill or ability.
The political **prowess** of Golda Meir made her an outstanding world leader.

rustic
rus´ tik

adj. 1. Of or relating to country life or people.
The pictures of grazing cows gave a certain **rustic** charm to the room.

2. Lacking elegance or polish.
A **rustic** cabin of rough-hewn logs was our home for the summer.

n. A country person, especially one thought of as simple or crude.
Shakespeare's **rustics** provide much of the humor in his comedies.

subtle
sut´ l

adj. 1. So slight as to be not easily seen or understood.
Jeff's **subtle** hints that he wanted a skateboard for his birthday went unnoticed by his parents.

2. Able to understand fine shades of meaning.
Corinne's **subtle** mind immediately saw a way to make the plan work.

subtlety *n.* Something so slight that only a clever or well-educated person can see it; the quality of being subtle.
The professor pointed out the **subtlety** of the poet's message in her later works.

vocation
vō kā´ shən

n. A person's employment; occupation.
Carpentry started out as my hobby but soon became my **vocation**.

vocational *adj.* Having to do with a person's career.
I learned my trade at the county **vocational** school.

warble   *v.* To sing in a melodious manner.

wôr´bəl   Somewhere in the gathering darkness, a nightingale began to **warble.**

15A ▶ **Finding Meanings**

Choose two phrases to form a sentence that correctly uses a word from Word List 15. Write each sentence in the space provided.

1. (a) To emphasize something is to   (c) deny it ever happened.
   (b) To warble something is to   (d) stress its importance.

   _____

   _____

2. (a) A subtle element is   (c) one that contributes to making up a whole.

   (b) A component element is   (d) one that can be easily replaced.

   _____

   _____

3. (a) sing it.   (c) To complement something is to
   (b) praise it.   (d) To warble something is to

   _____

   _____

4. (a) a state of doubt or uncertainty.   (c) Homage is
   (b) Prowess is   (d) honor paid in public.

   _____

   _____

5. (a) deals with career planning.   (c) A pretentious guide
   (b) A vocational guide   (d) deals with low-cost travel.

   _____

   _____

6. (a) that draws undue attention to itself.   (c) A rustic sign is one

   (b) that is in need of repair.   (d) A pretentious sign is one

   _____

   _____

7. (a) make light of it.
   (b) bring it to completion.

   (c) To complement something is to
   (d) To conjure up something is to

   _____

   _____

8. (a) A lush garden is one
   (b) A rustic garden is one

   (c) that is open to the public.
   (d) with a rich growth of vegetation.

   _____

   _____

9. (a) to do that person a favor.
   (b) make that person disappear.

   (c) To conjure up someone is
   (d) To oblige someone is

   _____

   _____

10. (a) An impromptu change
    (b) A subtle change

    (c) is one that is very slight.
    (d) is one that is unavoidable.

    _____

    _____

complement

component

conjure

emphasize

homage

impromptu

lush

medley

oblige

pretentious

prowess

rustic

subtle

vocation

warble

Improve each of the following sentences by crossing out the bold phrase and replacing it with a word (or a form of the word) from Word List 15.

1. Edith Wharton's novels are noted for their **fine qualities that may not be immediately obvious to the casual reader.**

2. This lace tablecloth is a perfect **finishing touch** to your fine china and silverware.

3. Pelé's **great skill** with a soccer ball made him a legendary figure.

4. Although he may look like a **simple country person,** my neighbor is a very astute businessperson.

5. Your mentioning lobsters **makes me think back and brings** up memories of that summer we spent in Maine.

6. In both our beginners' and advanced scuba diving courses, the **most important lesson that is taught** is on safety.

7. If you sign the application, you are **left with no choice and will be forced** to accept the offer.

8. The orchestra opened the concert with a **wide-ranging selection** of Broadway show tunes.

9. Politicians must be able to speak **without any preparation and without notes** on just about any subject.

10. Gardening was both her **chosen profession** and her hobby.

Circle the letter or letters of each correct answer. A question may have more than one correct answer.

1. Which of the following might be a **vocation?**
   - (a) teaching
   - (b) nursing
   - (c) napping
   - (d) flying

2. Which of the following would be a full **complement?**
   - (a) twelve eggs in a carton
   - (b) twenty-four checkers pieces
   - (c) seven baseball players
   - (d) fifty-two playing cards

3. Which of the following can be **conjured** up?
   - (a) a fond memory
   - (b) a piece of music
   - (c) a past event
   - (d) a line of poetry

4. To which of the following might we pay **homage?**
   - (a) an intrepid war hero
   - (b) a great writer
   - (c) an illustrious film actor
   - (d) a former president

5. Which of the following is a **rustic** scene?
   - (a) a Vermont covered bridge
   - (b) a Florida citrus grove
   - (c) a New Hampshire lake
   - (d) a New York skyscraper

6. Which of the following might be **subtle?**
   - (a) a suggestion
   - (b) a line of poetry
   - (c) a shift of mood
   - (d) a circus clown

7. Which of the following might **oblige** a person?
   - (a) making a promise
   - (b) accepting an offer
   - (c) borrowing money
   - (d) repaying a loan

8. Which of the following might be **lush?**
   - (a) a meadow
   - (b) a tropical rain forest
   - (c) a valley
   - (d) a desert

complement
component
conjure
emphasize
homage
impromptu
lush
medley
oblige
pretentious
prowess
rustic
subtle
vocation
warble

Complete the analogies by selecting the pair of words whose relationship most resembles the relationship of the pair in capital letters. Circle the letter of the pair you choose.

1. SKILL : PROWESS ::
   - (a) consternation : fear
   - (b) fire : smoke
   - (c) orbit : planet
   - (d) journey : destination

2. WARBLE : SONG ::
   - (a) applaud : discovery
   - (b) receive : gift
   - (c) invite : audience
   - (d) recite : poem

3. ZESTFUL : ENTHUSIASM ::
   - (a) menial : work
   - (b) acrid : smoke
   - (c) negligent : vigilance
   - (d) blithe : joy

4. STRAITS : HELP ::
   - (a) sphere : shape
   - (b) citrus : fruit
   - (c) tedium : excitement
   - (d) throng : congestion

5. ENDORSE : DISAPPROVE ::
   - (a) initiate : begin
   - (b) bestow : take
   - (c) placate : gratify
   - (d) smolder : burn

6. ABYSS : DITCH ::
   - (a) sea : land
   - (b) hole : open
   - (c) mountain : hill
   - (d) wound : doctor

7. ENLIGHTENED : IGNORANT ::
   - (a) industrious : lazy
   - (b) watchful : vigilant
   - (c) precise : exact
   - (d) irate : angry

8. VOCATIONAL : CAREER ::
   - (a) aquatic : water
   - (b) commit : crime
   - (c) steal : bestow
   - (d) borrow : money

9. MENAGERIE : ANIMALS ::
   - (a) sky : clouds
   - (b) theater : audience
   - (c) ocean : ships
   - (d) garden : plants

10. PLAUSIBLE : BELIEVABLE ::
    - (a) stringent : strict
    - (b) pretentious : humble
    - (c) scrupulous : lax
    - (d) preposterous : realistic

Read the passage. Then answer the questions that follow it.

Bluegrass

To horse lovers, the word *bluegrass* **conjures** up a picture of Kentucky's **lush** blue-green pastures, home of champion racehorses; but to lovers of country music, bluegrass is the lively sound of fiddles, banjos, mandolins, and guitars playing together in rapid foot-stompin', hand-clappin' harmony. Its roots go back many years to the Scottish and Irish immigrants who settled in the Appalachian region. These settlers brought their traditional tunes and songs with them. In the days before television, movies, and radio, families were **obliged** to supply their own entertainment. Anyone who could scrape a tune from a fiddle or **warble** a song would be invited to join in.

After the Civil War, newly freed Black slaves found jobs in Appalachia. They worked as coal miners, loggers, and railroad construction workers. They also introduced their music to the people of Appalachia, bringing in the "banjar," an African four-stringed instrument. The banjar was made from a hollowed gourd with a neck attached. Its twanging sound **complemented** the traditional fiddle so well that over time it was developed into the modern banjo. By the end of the nineteenth century, the guitar had been added, brought to Appalachia by city musicians traveling in bands through the region. All the **components** of bluegrass music were now in place. Its distinctive sound was beginning to emerge, although it did not yet have a name.

At first, the music coming out of Appalachia was ignored by most Americans who criticized its lack of **subtlety.** They thought of it as music that would appeal only to **rustics.** This impression was often created by the musicians themselves. They enjoyed combining slapstick comedy with their musical **medleys.** The coming of radio in the 1920s put more **emphasis** on the music itself and brought it a wider audience and more general acceptance. Together with recorded music, radio offered greater commercial opportunities. Musicians were no longer content to play the fiddle or the guitar merely as a hobby. More and more began to make music their **vocation.** Among them was Bill Monroe, who was born in western Kentucky in 1911. Bill showed his **prowess** with the mandolin at an early age. In 1938, he formed a band and named it after the nickname of his native state—the

complement
component
conjure
emphasize
homage
impromptu
lush
medley
oblige
pretentious
prowess
rustic
subtle
vocation
warble

Blue Grass Boys. Over the years that followed, the name of Monroe's band lent itself to the distinctive sound he had created.

A 2003 study showed an astonishing surge of interest in bluegrass. Eight million people had bought a bluegrass recording in the previous year. Bluegrass festivals are held in just about every state in the union and in many foreign countries. These musical events are not at all **pretentious;** in fact, performers mix freely with their fans. Those attending enjoy taking out their own instruments to join in **impromptu** performances held in any open space between campers. Many also come to pay **homage** to Bill Monroe, the father of bluegrass. Monroe and his Blue Grass Boys continued to perform until he was in his eighties, although he reduced the number of festival performances from 150 to 100 per year. On September 9, 1996, four days before his eighty-fifth birthday, Bill Monroe died.

▶ **Answer each of the following questions in the form of a sentence. If a question does not contain a vocabulary word from the lesson's word list, use one in your answer. Use each word only once.**

1. Why is Kentucky a good place to raise horses?

    _____

    _____

2. At what stage of his life did Bill Monroe first show his musical ability?

    _____

    _____

3. Why do many fans take their instruments to bluegrass festivals?

    _____

    _____

4. Who would be especially welcome at Appalachian get-togethers in the days before radio and television?

    _____

    _____

5. Why did the banjo become popular in Appalachian music?

    _____

    _____

6. To lovers of country music, what does the name *bluegrass* suggest?

_____

_____

7. How would you describe a **medley** of Bill Monroe tunes?

_____

_____

8. What is the meaning of **obliged** as it is used in the passage?

_____

_____

9. What instruments are one **component** of bluegrass music?

_____

_____

10. Why are fans able to mix freely with musicians at bluegrass festivals?

_____

_____

11. What mistaken idea did some Americans have about the appeal of bluegrass music?

_____

_____

complement
component
conjure
emphasize
homage
impromptu
lush
medley
oblige
pretentious
prowess
rustic
subtle
vocation
warble

12. What criticism might some lovers of "fine" music make of bluegrass music?

_____

_____

13. Why do you think the bluegrass musicians ultimately eliminated the slapstick comedy routines?

_____

_____

14. How did Bill Monroe demonstrate his devotion to country music?

_____

_____

15. What special purpose draws bluegrass fans to Bill Monroe's performances?

_____

_____

FUN & FASCINATING FACTS

Complement is a noun and a verb. *Compliment* (with an *i)* is also a noun and a verb, but these two words have quite different meanings. A *compliment* is a remark that expresses praise, approval, or admiration. To *compliment* someone is to make such a remark.

We sometimes refer to a person's profession, occupation, or chosen way of life as a *calling*. (Supreme Court Justice Ruth Bader Ginsburg has combined the *callings* of motherhood and the law.) *Calling* and **vocation** are synonyms, and this is no surprise because *vocation* comes from the Latin *vocare,* which means "to call." The prefix *a-* means "away from," and an *avocation* is a hobby or pastime, something done "away from" one's work or calling.

For more practice and games, go to **www.WordlyWise3000.com**.

| **Word List** | Study the definitions of the words. Then do the exercises that follow. |

bounty
boun´ tē

n. 1. A payment made as a reward, especially one made by the authorities.
The town offered a $25 **bounty** for each predatory animal that was killed.

2. That which is given freely, by nature or a generous person.
The people of Nova Scotia lived off the **bounty** of the sea.

bountiful *adj.* (boun´ ti fəl) Plentiful.
Farmers attributed the **bountiful** harvest to adequate rainfall throughout the growing season.

camouflage
kam´ ə fläzh

n. 1. The hiding of something as a result of its appearance.
The green color of a praying mantis is its natural means of **camouflage.**

2. Something used as a cover or disguise.
Netting covered with leafy branches provided **camouflage** for the trucks.

v. To hide or conceal, especially by disguising the appearance of.
Octopuses **camouflage** themselves by changing color to match their background.

ebb
eb

v. 1. To recede, fall back, or pull away from.
The rocks near the shore were exposed as the tide **ebbed.**

2. To fall to a lower level or weaker state; to dwindle.
The patient's strength had **ebbed** to the point where getting out of bed was an effort.

n. The passing to a lower level or weaker state.
Just when the shipwrecked sailors' hopes of rescue were at their lowest **ebb,** they saw a ship approaching the island.

forage
fôr´ ij

v. To search for food or supplies.
We **foraged** in the forest for firewood.

n. Food such as hay or grain for farm animals.
I supplement the horses' **forage** with carrots and apples.

harass
hə ras´

v. 1. To trouble or annoy by attacking repeatedly.
Swarms of mosquitoes **harassed** us as we left the tent.

2. To cause to become worried or weary.
The store owners were **harassed** by the rapid increase in shoplifting.

insulate in´ sə lāt	*v.* To cover with a material that keeps electricity, heat, or sound from escaping. The builder used fiberglass to **insulate** the walls.
	insulation *n.* Material that is used to insulate. Their down provides geese with **insulation** against the cold.
lethargic lə thär´ jik	*adj.* Slow moving; sleepy or tired. Extreme heat often makes people **lethargic.**
	lethargy *n.* (leth´ ər jē) A state of laziness, tiredness, or of not caring. Despite repeated pep talks from the coach, a **lethargy** had settled over the team.
maneuver mə nōō´ vər	*n.* 1. A planned military movement. A frontal attack on a well-defended position is not a **maneuver** I would recommend.
	2. A skillful move or clever trick. Sacrificing her bishop early in the chess game turned out to be an effective **maneuver.**
	v. 1. To perform military movements with. General Lee **maneuvered** his forces so skillfully that the outcome of the battle was never in doubt.
	2. To move or manage in a skillful way. The tugboats **maneuvered** the ship into position alongside the dock.
mottled mät´ əld	*adj.* Marked with different colored patches or blotches. The granite had a **mottled** pink and gray appearance.
murky mʉrk´ ē	*adj.* Dark; gloomy. I gazed over the side of the boat into the **murky** depths of the harbor.
proximity präk sim´ ə tē	*n.* The state of being close or next to; nearness. The lawyers looked for an office with **proximity** to the courthouse.
replenish rē plen´ ish	*v.* To fill up again. We **replenished** our water bottles at a little stream.
sleek slēk	*adj.* 1. Smooth and glossy. The dog's coat was **sleek** from daily brushing.
	2. Having slender, graceful lines. The **sleek** ocean liner was a beautiful sight.
wary wer´ ē	*adj.* On one's guard; watchful; suspicious. She advised me to be **wary** of the advertisement's claims.

wean
wēn

v. 1. To cause to stop depending on a mother's milk for nourishment. Puppies are **weaned** at six weeks.

2. To detach from something one has grown accustomed to. The cafeteria menu replaced doughnuts with a medley of fruits in an attempt to **wean** students away from sweets.

16A ▷ Finding Meanings

Choose two phrases to form a sentence that correctly uses a word from Word List 16. Write each sentence in the space provided.

1. (a) it is clear and straightforward.
   (b) If something is murky,
   (c) If something is mottled,
   (d) it is not very clear.

_____

_____

2. (a) bring them up to a needed level.
   (b) To camouflage supplies is to
   (c) save them for future use.
   (d) To replenish supplies is to

_____

_____

3. (a) A mottled coat is one
   (b) with blotches of different colors.
   (c) thick enough to keep out the cold.
   (d) A sleek coat is one

_____

_____

4. (a) Camouflage is
   (b) the act of concealment.
   (c) a state of inactivity.
   (d) Insulation is

_____

_____

5. (a) A wary child is one who
   (b) A lethargic child is one who
   (c) is lacking in self-confidence.
   (d) is watchful and suspicious.

_____

_____

6. (a) Forage is used to
   (b) replace what has been used up.
   (c) keep heat from escaping.
   (d) Insulation is used to

_____

_____

bounty
camouflage
ebb
forage
harass
insulate
lethargic
maneuver
mottled
murky
proximity
replenish
sleek
wary
wean

7. (a) slender and graceful.   (c) A sleek animal is one that is
   (b) A lethargic animal is one that is   (d) obedient and easily trained.

   _____

   _____

8. (a) Proximity is   (c) that which is given freely.
   (b) Bounty is   (d) that which has been lost.

   _____

   _____

9. (a) To maneuver is to   (c) pass the time aimlessly.
   (b) recede.   (d) To ebb is to

   _____

   _____

10. (a) quickness of movement.   (c) grass or grain that farm animals eat.
    (b) Forage is   (d) Proximity is

    _____

    _____

16B ▷ Just the Right Word

Improve each of the following sentences by crossing out the bold phrase and replacing it with a word (or a form of the word) from Word List 16.

1. In order to save energy, the hot-water tank had been **covered with a material that kept heat from escaping.**

2. The baby was **stopped from depending on its mother's milk** at six months.

3. My **slow-moving and sleepy** condition is caused by the medicine I'm taking for my flu.

4. Siamese cats have **smooth and glossy** coats.

5. The **planned military movement** was carried out promptly and swiftly.

6. The landlord began to **do annoying things to make trouble for** me when I refused to move out.

7. **How close it is** to public transportation can be an important factor in choosing a home.

8. After three days, the floodwaters started to **sink to a low level.**

9. Raccoons like to go **searching for something to eat** in the garbage cans.

10. The troops in the jungle **disguised the appearance of** themselves by wearing jackets with splotches of brown and green colors.

16c ▶ **Applying Meanings**

Circle the letter or letters of each correct answer. A question may have more than one correct answer.

1. Which places are in **proximity** to the United States?
   - (a) Mexico
   - (b) Tibet
   - (c) Turkey
   - (d) Canada

2. Which of the following could be **replenished?**
   - (a) a dwindling supply
   - (b) water bottles
   - (c) an emptied glass
   - (d) hunger

3. Which of the following are signs of **lethargy?**
   - (a) an exuberant manner
   - (b) daydreaming
   - (c) frequent naps
   - (d) strenuous exercise

4. On which of the following might there be a **bounty?**
   - (a) an outlaw
   - (b) a mythical animal
   - (c) a pet rabbit
   - (d) a rattlesnake

5. Which of the following might be used to **camouflage** a car?
   - (a) leafy branches
   - (b) tinted windows
   - (c) green and brown paint
   - (d) whitewall tires

6. Which of the following can **ebb?**
   - (a) the tide
   - (b) a person's hopes
   - (c) floodwaters
   - (d) interest in a project

bounty
camouflage
ebb
forage
harass
insulate
lethargic
maneuver
mottled
murky
proximity
replenish
sleek
wary
wean

7. Which of the following animals could be called **sleek?**
   (a) a dolphin   (c) a turtle
   (b) a greyhound   (d) a camel

8. Which of the following can be **maneuvered?**
   (a) test results   (c) a boat
   (b) a spacecraft   (d) an army

Word Study

Each group of four words contains either two synonyms or two antonyms. Circle that pair. Then circle the *S* if they are synonyms or the *A* if they are antonyms.

1. wary	bountiful	eerie	trusting	S	A
2. murky	lush	clear	aware	S	A
3. scanty	sleek	bountiful	cloudy	S	A
4. proximity	disguise	camouflage	movement	S	A
5. wavy	blotchy	mottled	lethargic	S	A
6. annoy	ebb	harass	arrange	S	A
7. energetic	sleek	lethargic	unsure	S	A
8. forage	rise	ebb	zest	S	A
9. replenish	wean	detach	oblige	S	A
10. movement	insulation	maneuver	reaction	S	A

Read the passage. Then answer the questions that follow it.

Harbor Seals

Because they live in close **proximity** to the shore, harbor seals are a familiar sight along the New England coast. You may have to look closely to see them because their coloring provides them with a good **camouflage;** their gray and black **mottled** coats are hard to see against the seaweed-covered rocks on which they spend much of their time. During the winter months, they inhabit the waters around Cape Cod and along the Massachusetts shoreline. Their dense fur and thick layer of blubber keep them so well **insulated** that in summer they seek the colder waters of Maine and the Atlantic provinces of Canada.

Harbor seals are equally at home on land and in the water. As the tide **ebbs,** they climb onto rocks along the shoreline. They return to the water at high tide to **forage** for crabs, fish, and squid. Harbor seals may seem **lethargic** as they lie basking in the sun, but actually they are **replenishing** their blood supply with fresh oxygen. Whether hunting for food or escaping from sharks and killer whales, harbor seals burn up oxygen rapidly when they are in the water.

Because of their **sleek** bodies and powerful rear flippers, harbor seals can swim up to fifteen miles an hour. They can also **maneuver** swiftly. They use their front flippers to brake and steer. Their excellent eyesight is necessary for survival. Harbor seals must watch for predators in the **murky** New England waters. Healthy harbor seals that stay out of harm's way can live for thirty years.

An adult harbor seal weighs over 200 pounds and eats up to twenty pounds of fish a day. This makes the seals unpopular with those who fish for a living. In fact, seals were so unpopular in the 1800s that the state of Maine offered a **bounty** of five dollars for every harbor seal killed. Then the Marine Mammal Protection Act of 1972 made harbor seals a protected species. The Act was updated in 1994. It is now against the law to kill, capture, or **harass** them in any way.

Female harbor seals give birth in late May and early June. Newborn pups weigh about twenty pounds. They feed on their mother's milk until they are **weaned** at six to eight weeks. Within hours of being born, they are able to swim and are completely at home in the water. Young seals stay close to their

bounty
camouflage
ebb
forage
harass
insulate
lethargic
maneuver
mottled
murky
proximity
replenish
sleek
wary
wean

mothers. The mothers keep a **wary** eye on them until they are able to take care of themselves.

Some seals who ran into problems can be seen by visitors to the New England Aquarium in Boston. Sick or injured seals that could not survive in the wild are brought there for medical treatment. They are kept in a holding tank outside the building. Once restored to health, the harbor seals are released into the ocean to enjoy its limitless freedom but also to face whatever dangers lurk there.

▶ **Answer each of the following questions in the form of a sentence. If a question does not contain a vocabulary word from the lesson's word list, use one in your answer. Use each word only once.**

1. Why are harbor seals unlikely to be spotted in midocean?

_____

_____

2. What happens to the tide when it reaches the high-water mark?

_____

_____

3. Are harbor seals **lethargic** in the water?

_____

_____

4. Which single word describes both the body shape and coat of the harbor seal?

_____

_____

5. What is the meaning of **camouflage** as it is used in the passage?

_____

_____

6. Why do you need sharp eyes to see harbor seals basking on the rocks?

_____

_____

7. What is the meaning of **bounty** as it is used in the passage?

_____

_____

8. Why are harbor seals sometimes difficult to spot in the water?

_____

_____

9. Why do harbor seals spend so much time lying in the sun?

_____

_____

10. How does the passage show that seals are good mothers?

_____

_____

11. Why is it difficult for predators to catch harbor seals?

_____

_____

12. What is the purpose of the harbor seal's thick layer of blubber?

_____

_____

bounty

camouflage

ebb

forage

harass

insulate

lethargic

maneuver

mottled

murky

proximity

replenish

sleek

wary

wean

13. How do mature harbor seals obtain the nourishment they need?

_____

_____

14. How does the law protect harbor seals?

_____

_____

15. What is the meaning of **wean** as it is used in the passage?

_____

_____

FUN & FASCINATING FACTS

- **Camouflage** is a French military term that has entered English while retaining its original French spelling and pronunciation.

- **Harass** is sometimes pronounced *ha rass'* and sometimes *har' ess*. While both pronunciations are correct, the second is considered preferable by many dictionaries.

- In some situations, **ebb** and *flow* are antonyms. For example, we speak of the ebb and flow or falling and rising of the tide. (The science teacher explained that the tide *ebbs* and *flows* twice approximately every twenty-four hours.)

Crossword Puzzle Solve the crossword puzzle by studying the clues and filling in the answer boxes. Clues followed by a number are definitions of words in Lessons 13 through 16. The number gives the word list in which the answer to the clue appears.

Clues Across

1. Extremely gloomy or depressing (14)
4. The _____ Canal is in Egypt.
8. On one's guard (16)
9. Too absurd to be believed (14)
11. Eight, nine, _____
12. In addition to; as well as
16. Producing wealth or profit (13)
17. Suggesting the country or country life (15)
19. One's occupation, trade, or career (15)
21. Sun, _____ , and stars
23. To do a favor for (15)
24. A mixture of dissimilar things (15)
26. The highest point (13)
27. To give one's backing to (13)
28. To start burning (13)

Clues Down

2. Glossy and smooth (16)
3. Growing thick and healthy (15)
4. Trouble or need (13)
5. Keen enjoyment (13)
6. To cause to become worried (16)
7. We see with them
10. Showing no fear (13)
13. Not easily seen or understood (15)
14. A bow and _____
15. Very great skill or ability (15)
18. To make appear as if by magic (15)
20. Food for farm animals (16)
21. A wise friend and adviser (13)
22. Showing a childish lack of judgment (14)
25. To lie in wait as though about to attack (14)

For more practice and games, go to **www.WordlyWise3000.com**.

| **Word List** | Study the definitions of the words. Then do the exercises that follow. |

appoint
ə point´

v. 1. To choose for an office or position.
The president **appoints** justices to the Supreme Court.

2. To set or decide upon.
Let's **appoint** a time for our next meeting.

appointment *n.* 1. The act of appointing or being appointed.
All **appointments** to the Supreme Court must be approved by Congress.

2. An arrangement or agreement to meet.
I made an **appointment** to see the editor on Thursday at 3:00 P.M.

assent
ə sent´

v. To give one's consent; to agree.
The members of the union **assented** to the terms of the new contract.

n. An act of agreeing or acceptance.
Congress gave its **assent** to the new welfare reform bill.

concur
kən kʉr´

v. To be in agreement.
Dr. Alvarez **concurred** with Dr. Yan's opinion that the patient did not require surgery.

consult
kən sult´

v. 1. To seek information or advice.
I **consulted** several reference books to get information about asteroids hitting the earth.

2. To talk things over in order to reach a decision.
While court went into recess, the lawyers **consulted** each other.

consultation *n.* (kän səl tā´ shən) A discussion; a meeting to seek advice.
The first **consultation** with an attorney is often free.

consultant *n.* One whose advice is sought.
The city manager hired a **consultant** to advise her on care for the elderly.

dissuade
di swād´

v. To prevent or discourage someone from doing something.
My friend **dissuaded** me from skiing the trail called White Heat.

flabbergast
flab´ ər gast

v. To surprise so greatly that one is speechless; to amaze.
His preposterous story about being abducted by space aliens **flabbergasted** me.

haggle
hag´ əl

v. To argue about, especially about the price of something.
We **haggled** with the dealer for a while before agreeing on a price for the painting.

perturb pər tʉrb´	*v.* To make uneasy; to upset greatly. I was **perturbed** when the plane's late departure caused me to miss the business meeting.
procure prō kyoor´	*v.* To get by making an effort; to obtain. By foraging in the woods, I was able to **procure** enough kindling to start a fire.
receptive rē sep´ tiv	*adj.* Ready and able to receive ideas or suggestions. The Senate was **receptive** to the president's plan for more aid to the cities.
repudiate rē pyōo´ dē āt	*v.* To refuse to support; to reject. New discoveries often cause scientists to **repudiate** earlier beliefs.
resolve rē zôlv´	*v.* 1. To make a firm promise to oneself. I **resolve** to work even harder at my studies. 2. To solve. We can **resolve** this little problem very easily. *n.* A fixed purpose or intention. The hard toil and long days weakened Tom's **resolve** to finish the job.
signify sig´ nə fī	*v.* 1. To be a sign of; to mean. A nod of the head **signifies** agreement. 2. To make known or clear. **Signify** your approval of the proposed change by raising your hand. **significant** *adj.* (sig nif´ ə kənt) Full of meaning; important. "There was no forced entry. That is very **significant**," said the detective. **significance** *n.* (sig nif´ ə kəns) Importance; meaning. What is the **significance** of flying the flag upside down?
sovereign säv´ rən	*adj.* 1. Highest; chief. Clearness of expression is a **sovereign** quality in writing. 2. Not controlled by others. After winning independence from England, the thirteen colonies formed a **sovereign** country. *n.* A king or queen; a monarch. The **sovereign's** portrait appears on all British postage stamps. **sovereignty** *n.* Freedom from political control by a foreign power. Poland regained its **sovereignty** when the Soviet Union collapsed at the end of the Cold War.
trifling trī´ fliŋ	*adj.* Of little value, importance, or meaning. Their objections to the plan are **trifling** and should be ignored.

Choose two phrases to form a sentence that correctly uses a word from Word List 17. Write each sentence in the space provided.

1. (a) To repudiate something
   (b) To resolve something
   (c) is to settle it.
   (d) is to be the cause of it.

_____

_____

2. (a) To perturb someone is to
   (b) make that person uneasy.
   (c) To consult someone is to
   (d) reject that person.

_____

_____

3. (a) refuse to be bound by it.
   (b) sign one's name to it.
   (c) To procure an agreement is to
   (d) To repudiate an agreement is to

_____

_____

4. (a) An appointment is
   (b) A consultation is
   (c) a matter of little importance.
   (d) the naming of a person to a position.

_____

_____

5. (a) is to be a sign of change.
   (b) is to be unwilling to accept change.
   (c) To assent to change
   (d) To signify change

_____

_____

6. (a) A trifling figure is one
   (b) that has no real existence.
   (c) A sovereign figure is one
   (d) that stands out above all others.

_____

_____

7. (a) be unable to make up one's mind.
   (b) To concur is to
   (c) be in agreement.
   (d) To haggle is to

_____

_____

8. (a) To flabbergast someone
   (b) is to welcome that person.
   (c) To dissuade someone
   (d) is to amaze that person.

_____

_____

9. (a) is to give it up.   (c) To procure something
   (b) is to obtain it.   (d) To assent to something

_____

_____

10. (a) Someone who is dissuaded   (c) is ready to accept new ideas.
    (b) Someone who is receptive   (d) is unwilling to consider new ideas.

_____

_____

17B   Just the Right Word

Improve each of the following sentences by crossing out the bold phrase and replacing it with a word (or a form of the word) from Word List 17.

1. I was able to **obtain through my own efforts** forage for the horses.

2. My parents' sound objections weakened my **firm intention** to join the club.

3. Belize, formerly British Honduras, gained **freedom from political control by another country** in 1981.

4. The **meeting in which I talked things over** with the doctor lasted thirty minutes.

5. I **indicated that I was willing to give my approval** to the proposal.

6. Let's not waste our time on such **completely unimportant** matters.

7. A vote of 9 to 0 **makes it clear** that the decision was unanimous.

8. I paid what the car salesperson asked since I was unwilling to **argue over the price.**

9. I tried to **use my powers of persuasion in order to prevent** them from driving in such icy conditions.

10. All the relatives gathered in the lawyer's office for the **meeting that had been arranged the week before.**

appoint
assent
concur
consult
dissuade
flabbergast
haggle
perturb
procure
receptive
repudiate
resolve
signify
sovereign
trifling

Circle the letter or letters of each correct answer. A question may have more than one correct answer.

1. Which of the following would result in a country's loss of **sovereignty?**
   (a) It closes off its borders.
   (b) It abolishes its army.
   (c) It is overrun by a foreign power.
   (d) Its citizens overthrow the ruler.

2. Which of the following might a person **resolve** to do?
   (a) drive more carefully
   (b) catch a cold
   (c) stop smoking
   (d) start smoking

3. Which of the following might be **haggled** over?
   (a) the terms of an agreement
   (b) the price of an antique
   (c) the day on which Thanksgiving falls
   (d) the number of feet in a mile

4. Which of the following might **perturb** a businessperson?
   (a) increased competition
   (b) increased taxes
   (c) increased profits
   (d) increased expenses

5. Which of the following are ways of **assenting?**
   (a) nodding one's head
   (b) saying yes
   (c) saying no
   (d) shaking one's head

6. Which of the following could be **appointed?**
   (a) a club president
   (b) a cabinet member
   (c) a place to meet
   (d) a winter storm

7. Which of the following have **significance?**
   (a) a sudden weight loss
   (b) lethargy after a large meal
   (c) a presidential election
   (d) the color of one's eyes

8. Which of the following can be **consulted?**
   (a) a dictionary
   (b) a mentor
   (c) an authority
   (d) an accountant

Combine the prefixes and Latin words to make eight words. The boldface word (or words) in each sentence is a direct clue to help you figure out part or all of the word. The numbers in parentheses give the word list from which each word is taken.

Prefixes
com- (together)
in- (not)
inter- (between)
re- (again)
sub- (under)

Latin Words
mergere (to plunge)   vincere (to conquer)
plenus (full)   placare (to calm)
proximus (near)   ponere (to put)
trepidus (afraid)   venire (to come)

1. Several of these **put together** make a whole.

   They are _____ . (15)

2. This is what you do to **calm** hurt feelings.

   You _____ someone. (9)

3. Can't be **conquered?**

   You are _____ ! (9)

4. Diving **under** the surface?

   You're going to _____ yourself. (11)

5. You're getting **near** the park.

   You're in _____ to it now! (16)

6. You can **fill** your tank **again.**

   The word is _____ . (16)

7. Don't want to **come between** friends?

   Then don't _____ . (12)

8. Don't be **afraid!**

   Be _____ . (13)

appoint

assent

concur

consult

dissuade

flabbergast

haggle

perturb

procure

receptive

repudiate

resolve

signify

sovereign

trifling

Read the passage. Then answer the questions that follow it.

"A Noble Bargain"

Throughout history, countries that have extended their borders have done so mainly by military conquest; the United States is one of the few nations that has ever done so by purchase. In one of the greatest bargains ever made, it **procured** almost a million square miles at a cost of just over fifteen million dollars.

In 1802, the **sovereignty** of the United States ended at the Mississippi River. France had a legal claim to all the land beyond it as far as the Rocky Mountains. United States shipping on the Mississippi passed through New Orleans, Louisiana, on its way to the sea. President Thomas Jefferson was **perturbed** by the possibility that France might close off the river. To prevent this, he **resolved** to buy New Orleans, together with western Florida, from the French.

Certain conditions were in Jefferson's favor. France was on the verge of war with Britain and, therefore, needed money. Should the British attack New Orleans, the French would, Jefferson believed, have difficulty defending it. It made sense to conclude that France would prefer the territory go to America rather than to Britain.

To pursue his plan, Jefferson **appointed** two agents to represent the United States. These agents met with the French foreign minister in France to discuss the purchase. He proposed that the United States buy all the land from the Mississippi to the Rockies, a total of almost a million square miles. The two Americans were **flabbergasted** but **receptive** to the idea. Congress had approved spending only two million dollars; however, the cost would now greatly exceed that amount. After a considerable amount of **haggling,** a price of fifteen million dollars was finally agreed on. The French foreign minister commented at the time the deal was struck that the United States had made "a noble bargain."

Members of Congress did not **concur** with this view and wanted to **repudiate** the agreement with France. They thought that fifteen million dollars was an excessive amount to pay. They were also upset that the president's agents had agreed to the French offer without **consulting** them. President Jefferson appeared before Congress in an attempt to **dissuade** its members from voting against the purchase. He pointed out that the United

States would be doubled in size by the transaction. He also stated that if the United States did not act promptly, the French might withdraw their offer. Somewhat grudgingly, Congress gave its **assent** to the "Louisiana Purchase." A year later the United States flag was raised in New Orleans, **signifying** the end of France's involvement in North America.

Just how good a bargain was the Louisiana Purchase? Iowa farmland in 2003 sold for about $2,500 an acre. The six hundred million acres of land the United States bought in 1803 had cost the **trifling** sum of two and a half cents an acre.

▶ **Answer each of the following questions in the form of a sentence. If a question does not contain a vocabulary word from the lesson's word list, use one in your answer. Use each word only once.**

1. Why is 1803 a **significant** date in French history?

   _____

   _____

2. How did Jefferson feel about the possibility that France might close off the Mississippi River?

   _____

   _____

3. Why would it be incorrect to call Florida a **sovereign** state in 1802?

   _____

   _____

4. What decision did Jefferson make to ensure that the Mississippi River stayed open?

   _____

   _____

5. Did Jefferson himself deal directly with the French?

   _____

   _____

6. Why would it have been difficult for the agents to **consult** with Congress?

   _____

   _____

appoint
assent
concur
consult
dissuade
flabbergast
haggle
perturb
procure
receptive
repudiate
resolve
signify
sovereign
trifling

7. How do you know that the French proposal was unexpected?

_____

_____

8. How did the Americans make sure they paid no more than necessary?

_____

_____

9. Why might the Americans have pretended at first not to be **receptive** to the French offer?

_____

_____

10. How much land did the United States purchase from France?

_____

_____

11. What was the cost per square mile of the Louisiana Purchase?

_____

_____

12. Did everyone agree that the two Americans had performed a great service?

_____

_____

13. What was the purpose of Jefferson's address to the members of Congress?

_____

_____

14. What would have happened if Congress had **repudiated** the agreement?

_____

_____

15. What was Congress's response to Jefferson's appeal?

_____

_____

- The antonym of **assent** is *dissent;* its homophone is *ascent,* "the act of climbing or ascending."

- The noun formed from the verb **resolve** is *resolution*—one may *resolve* to do something; one may also make a *resolution* to do something. *Resolve* is also a noun, and its meaning overlaps somewhat with *resolution. Resolve* is a state of mind and means "firmness of purpose." (Nothing could shake her *resolve* to be a doctor.) A *resolution* is a statement of purpose, made to oneself or to others, concerning a course of action. (I made a New Year's *resolution* to exercise every day.) *Resolution* also means "an explanation or a solution." (The *resolution* of the mystery is withheld until the end of the novel.)

- **Sovereign** is formed from the Latin *super,* which means "over" or "above." As a noun, *sovereign* is a synonym for *monarch,* and the fact that a monarch *reigns* influenced the present form and spelling of the word. The noun formed from the adjective is *sovereignty.* (By world agreement, no country may claim *sovereignty* over Antarctica.)

A *sovereign* is also a British gold coin no longer in use; the first ones were struck in 1489 and bore a likeness of the English king Henry VII.

- The noun *trifle* is related to the adjective **trifling.** A trifle is something of little value or importance; it is also a sum of money so small as to be of no account. *Trifle* is also a verb that means "to talk or deal with in an insincere way." (Only an unscrupulous person would *trifle* with someone's affections.)

---

appoint

assent

concur

consult

dissuade

flabbergast

haggle

perturb

procure

receptive

repudiate

resolve

signify

sovereign

trifling

| **Word List** | Study the definitions of the words. Then do the exercises that follow. |

acclaim
ə klām´

v. To praise strongly or applaud loudly.
Car magazines have **acclaimed** the Z202's performance.

n. Strong praise or loud applause; approval.
The musicians from China won the critic's **acclaim** last night at Symphony Hall.

bigot
big´ ət

n. One who is not tolerant of those people who are different in some way; a prejudiced person.
Only a **bigot** would claim that one race is superior to another.

bigotry *n.* The intolerant attitude or behavior of such a person.
In one of their songs, the Beatles asked listeners to imagine a world free of **bigotry.**

covet
kuv´ ət

v. To have a strong and envious desire for, especially for something belonging to another.
The cattle ranchers **coveted** the lush pastures where the shepherds grazed their flocks.

coveted *adj.* Greatly prized; highly desired.
Former President Jimmy Carter won the **coveted** Nobel Peace Prize in 2002.

deceased
dē sēst´

adj. Dead.
The man's thoughts often turned to his **deceased** wife.

n. (with *the*) One who has died recently.
The funeral director asked if I was a relative of the **deceased.**

formidable
fôr´ mə də bəl

adj. 1. Causing fear or apprehension.
A team with a fourteen-game winning streak is a **formidable** opponent.

2. Difficult.
Crossing the Rocky Mountains was a **formidable** task for settlers heading west.

ghetto
get´ ō

n. A section of a city occupied by a minority group of people, usually because of poverty or social pressure.
The Warsaw **ghetto** in Poland was the location of the largest uprising during World War II.

momentous
mō men´ təs

adj. Very important.
The day of high school graduation is a **momentous** one for students.

oppress
ə pres´

v. 1. To weigh down with worry.
Fears of job layoffs **oppressed** workers in the auto industry.

2. To keep down by severe and unjust use of force.
According to the Bible story, the Egyptian pharaoh **oppressed** the Israelite slaves until Moses led them to freedom.

oppression *n.* (ə presh´ ən) The act or state of being oppressed.
The **oppression** of African Americans led to the Civil Rights Movement of the 1950s and '60s.

oppressive *adj.* Very harsh or burdensome.
This **oppressive** heat makes one very lethargic.

overwhelm
ō vər hwelm´

v. 1. To defeat utterly and completely.
Sioux and Cheyenne warriors **overwhelmed** General Custer's army at the Battle of Little Big Horn in 1876.

2. To deeply affect the mind or emotions of.
We were **overwhelmed** by the welcome we received.

3. To upset; to turn over.
A huge wave **overwhelmed** the small boat.

overwhelming *adj.* Great in strength or effect.
The union vote was an **overwhelming** 98 to 17 in favor of ending the strike.

perceive
pər sēv´

v. 1. To become aware of through the senses, especially the sense of sight.
I **perceived** a figure in the distance but could not make out who it was.

2. To take in information through the mind.
I **perceived** a subtle shift in their attitude.

perception *n.* (pər sep´ shən) The act of perceiving or the thing perceived.
Because I am farsighted, my **perception** of close objects is slightly fuzzy.

premiere
prē mir´

n. The first showing of a play, film, etc.
The play, a big success in London, has its North American **premiere** this Saturday.

prospective
prä spek´ tiv

adj. Expected or likely to happen or become.
The **prospective** bride wants to have a June wedding.

spurn
spʉrn

v. To refuse in a scornful way.
I **spurned** their offer of help because there were too many conditions attached to it.

staunch
stônch

adj. Faithful; true; strong.
Mr. Fielding, a **staunch** supporter of Little League baseball, donated the uniforms for our team.

theme *n.* 1. A dominant idea, as in art, literature, or music; a topic or subject.
thēm The **theme** of the story is the danger of excessive pride.

2. A short essay on a single subject.
I had to write a **theme** on ambition.

3. A series of musical notes on which variations are made; a melody that is associated with a film or television show.
The concert began with a medley of **themes** from popular television shows.

18A ▷ Finding Meanings

Choose two phrases to form a sentence that correctly uses a word from Word List 18. Write each sentence in the space provided.

1. (a) A momentous victory is
   (b) A prospective victory is
   (c) one that stands out from all others.
   (d) one that was gained unfairly.

   _____

   _____

2. (a) be impossible to defeat.
   (b) To be oppressed is to
   (c) To be acclaimed is to
   (d) receive high praise.

   _____

   _____

3. (a) to become aware of it.
   (b) To spurn a position is
   (c) To covet a position is
   (d) to want it very badly.

   _____

   _____

4. (a) The theme of a TV series is
   (b) the melody associated with it.
   (c) its reception by the critics.
   (d) The premiere of a movie is

   _____

   _____

5. (a) A ghetto is
   (b) A bigot is
   (c) someone who is intolerant of those who are different.
   (d) a remark that shows one is lacking in good manners.

   _____

   _____

6. (a) lose possession of it.   (c) To perceive something is to
   (b) To spurn something is to   (d) refuse it scornfully.

_____

_____

7. (a) one who is actively involved.   (c) A deceased partner is
   (b) A prospective partner is   (d) one who has died.

_____

_____

8. (a) To overwhelm a nation is to   (c) join forces with it.
   (b) To oppress a nation is to   (d) keep it down by force.

_____

_____

9. (a) A ghetto is   (c) a section of a city occupied
                       by a minority group.
   (b) A premiere is   (d) a short essay on a single subject.

_____

_____

10. (a) To overwhelm a problem is to   (c) become aware of it.
    (b) To perceive a problem is to   (d) be defeated by it.

_____

_____

18B ▷ Just the Right Word

Improve each of the following sentences by crossing out the bold phrase and replacing it with a word (or a form of the word) from Word List 18.

1. The problems we face are **very difficult and will not be solved easily.**

2. The collapse of Communism ended the seventy-year **weighing down by force** of the Russian people.

3. The **person who has just died** was one of my grandparents' oldest friends.

4. The governor was mentioned as a **person who might be nominated as a** member of the Supreme Court.

5. Justice Thurgood Marshall was a **strong and faithful** defender of civil rights for all Americans.

6. Alcohol distorts our **ability to obtain a clear picture** of what is happening around us.

7. I submitted a **short piece of writing** on the power of love to change people's lives.

8. Over the years, the United States has passed laws in an attempt to combat **intolerant attitudes directed against those who belong to different racial or ethnic groups.**

9. The movie's **first public showing** was attended by Hollywood's most glamorous stars.

10. I was **deeply affected emotionally** by my friends' generosity.

18C ▶ **Applying Meanings**

Circle the letter or letters of each correct answer. A question may have more than one correct answer.

1. Which of the following might have a **premiere?**
   (a) a new play
   (b) a new movie
   (c) a new building
   (d) a new law

2. Which of the following might someone **covet?**
   (a) a neighbor's new car
   (b) good health
   (c) a reprimand
   (d) a friend's job

3. Which of the following can be **spurned?**
   (a) a suggestion
   (b) ill health
   (c) a privilege
   (d) an invitation

4. Which of the following can have a **theme?**
   (a) a novel
   (b) a poem
   (c) a word
   (d) a painting

5. Which of the following can be **perceived?**
   - (a) the answer to a problem
   - (b) a ship on the horizon
   - (c) a threat
   - (d) loneliness

6. Which of the following might **overwhelm** a person?
   - (a) a grievous loss
   - (b) an arduous task
   - (c) a ruthless enemy
   - (d) a trifling matter

7. Which of the following can be **formidable?**
   - (a) opposition
   - (b) a kitten
   - (c) a journey
   - (d) a color

8. Which of the following can be **acclaimed?**
   - (a) lost property
   - (b) a victory
   - (c) a result
   - (d) a book

18D   Word Study

Sometimes words are easy to confuse because they sound similar. Read the pairs of sentences. Then choose the word that belongs in each sentence.

acclaim
bigot
covet
deceased
formidable
ghetto
momentous
oppress
overwhelm
perceive
premiere
prospective
spurn
staunch
theme

loath / loathe

1. The cat was _____ to leave her comfy spot by the fire.

2. "I _____ these New England winters," said Sally.

menial / manual

3. _____ workers get more exercise than office workers.

4. Many people have to do _____ work at their first job.

complement / compliment

5. The plum sauce is a nice _____ to the roast duck.

6. I gave a _____ to the chef for such a fine dish.

pander / ponder

7. The candidate said he would not _____ to the public.

8. While you _____ what to do next, your opponent acts.

principle / principal

9. Bananas are the _____ export of Central America.

10. The _____ of "one person, one vote" must be upheld.

horde / hoard

11. Aunt May likes to _____ her money and rarely spends a dollar.

12. A _____ of celebrating soccer fans rushed onto the field.

wary / weary

13. We were too _____ to eat and wished only to sleep.

14. Be _____ of advertisements that promise to make you rich.

momentous / momentary

15. January 1, 1863 was a _____ day in U.S. history.

16. Roller coasters provide _____ excitement.

vocation / vacation

17. We took our _____ in Mexico this year.

18. Poetry was Robert Frost's hobby and his _____ .

Read the passage. Then answer the questions that follow it.

An American Classic

Lorraine Hansberry's play *A Raisin in the Sun* opened in New York on March 11, 1959. It was a **momentous** day in the history of the American theater. *A Raisin in the Sun* was the first play written by an African American woman to appear on Broadway. It opened up the American theater to African Americans and broadened people's **perceptions** of the African American experience in society.

The reviews were **overwhelmingly** favorable. Even its **staunchest** supporters could not have predicted the impact the play would have on the American theater. It went on to win the **coveted** New York Drama Critics Circle award for Best Play of the Year. The opposition for the award was **formidable,** including works by two of America's greatest playwrights, Tennessee Williams and Eugene O'Neill.

A Raisin in the Sun is about African Americans confronting **oppression** in their daily lives. It was a **theme** that Hansberry was painfully familiar with in her own life. In 1938, her parents bought a house in an all-white neighborhood. The **bigotry** of their new neighbors resulted in a legal battle over property rights. A lower court ordered the Hansberrys to move out. They fought the case all the way to the U.S. Supreme Court and won, but the family suffered terribly in the process. Prejudice quickly escalated into violence. When Lorraine was eight years old, she was almost killed by a concrete slab thrown by an angry neighbor; it narrowly missed her head.

Hansberry's play tells the story of Lena Younger, who has received ten thousand dollars from her recently **deceased** husband's life insurance. Her dream is to move her family of five out of their cramped and rundown apartment in Chicago's South Side **ghetto.** She wants to use the money to buy a home in a white neighborhood, but doing that is not so simple.

Mrs. Younger is pressured by her son Walter to give him the money to improve his own financial state. Walter wants to invest in a liquor store. At the same time, her daughter Beneatha needs money; her dream is to attend medical school. Mrs. Younger decides to try to keep the family together by making a down payment on a house with about one-third of the money. She gives the remaining sum to Walter under the condition that he set aside $3,000 for his sister's tuition; the rest he may use as he wishes.

acclaim

bigot

covet

deceased

formidable

ghetto

momentous

oppress

overwhelm

perceive

premiere

prospective

spurn

staunch

theme

Before the family moves in, a **prospective** white neighbor contacts Mrs. Younger and explains that he is speaking for the entire neighborhood. He offers to buy back the house at a handsome profit for Mrs. Younger. Recognizing the offer as one motivated by blatant racism, she **spurns** it.

Matters soon get even more complicated. The family learns that Walter's business partner has cheated him out of the remaining money. The amount that was supposed to go toward Beneatha's education is gone.

The play ends with Mrs. Younger holding firm against all pressures and finding the courage to face new ones. The family will move into the all-white neighborhood, with all its problems, dangers, and opportunities.

A Raisin in the Sun ran for 533 performances on Broadway. Touring companies took it all over America, offering opportunities for black actors on a scale never known before. African Americans turned out in huge numbers to see a major American play that addressed the plight of minorities trying to improve their lives. In 1984, twenty-five years after its Broadway **premiere,** the play was performed at the Kennedy Center in Washington, D.C., and was shown on public television. By then it had won unanimous **acclaim** as an American classic.

▶ **Answer each of the following questions in the form of a sentence. If a question does not contain a vocabulary word from the lesson's word list, use one in your answer. Use each word only once.**

1. In what year did *A Raisin in the Sun* open on Broadway?

   _____

   _____

2. What effect did *A Raisin in the Sun* have on people?

   _____

   _____

3. What is the meaning of **theme** as it is used in the passage?

   _____

   _____

4. Why was March 11, 1959, a **momentous** day in the history of the American theater?

   _____

   _____

5. What important award did the play win?

_____

_____

6. Why must winning the award have given Lorraine Hansberry special satisfaction?

_____

_____

7. Why might it have been difficult to get tickets to see the play?

_____

_____

8. What might **staunch** supporters of the play have done to help it succeed?

_____

_____

9. Why is the person making the offer to buy the house from Mrs. Younger described as a **prospective** neighbor?

_____

_____

10. How does the passage show that Mrs. Younger scorns the offer?

_____

_____

11. What sort of person is the neighor who offers to buy back the house from Mrs. Younger?

_____

_____

12. How does Mrs. Younger deal with the **oppression** she encounters?

_____

_____

13. Why does Mr. Younger not appear in the play?

_____

_____

14. Why were many African Americans able to identify with the play's message?

_____

_____

acclaim

bigot

covet

deceased

formidable

ghetto

momentous

oppress

overwhelm

perceive

premiere

prospective

spurn

staunch

theme

15. What status had the play achieved by 1984?

_____

_____

FUN & FASCINATING FACTS

• The verb **covet** should not be confused with the adjective _covert_, which means "hidden." (I stole a _covert_ glance at the letter, trying to read the signature.)

• The adjectives **deceased** and _dead_ are synonyms, but note that _deceased_ refers only to human beings. It is often used to soften the harshness of death. ("My _deceased_ husband" falls more gently on the ear than "my _dead_ husband.") _Dead_ is the more general term and is applied to any living creature or figuratively to other things. (The bill is _dead_ unless the president can find six more senators to support it.)

• Don't confuse **premiere** with _premier_, an adjective meaning "first in position or importance." (The _pre-_ _mier_ cabinet positions are the Secretary of State, the Secretary of the Treasury, the Secretary of Defense, and the Attorney General.) _Premier_ is also a noun and means "the chief officer in a parliamentary system." (Winston Churchill was the _premier_ of Britain during the darkest days of World War Two.)

• In addition to its adjective form, **staunch** has a verb form meaning "to stop the flow of." _Stanch_ is a verb with the same meaning. (Pressure applied to a wound will _stanch_ the flow of blood.)

Confusion arises because as verbs these two words can be used interchangeably; however, only _stanch_ has an adjective form.

For more practice and games, go to www.WordlyWise3000.com.

Word List	Study the definitions of the words. Then do the exercises that follow.

adverse
ad vʉrs´

adj. 1. Working against; serving to oppose.
The response to the proposed parking ban was so **adverse** that the city council dropped the idea.

2. Harmful; unfavorable.
Some people have an **adverse** reaction to aspirin.

aloof
ə lōof´

adj. Remote or distant, usually by choice; showing no interest.
His **aloof** manner kept us from becoming close friends.

adv. In an aloof manner.
Although he sat with the group, he stayed **aloof** from the discussion they were having.

alternative
ôl tʉr´ nə tiv

adj. Allowing a choice between two or more things.
There is an **alternative** route you could take to get to town, but it's a bit longer.

n. 1. A choice between two or more things.
Your **alternatives** are to come with us or stay home.

2. Any one of the things that can be chosen.
I chose the second **alternative** and stayed home.

canine
kā´ nīn

adj. Of, or relating to, dogs or related animals.
Wolves, foxes, dogs, jackals, and coyotes are members of the **canine** family.

n. A member of the canine family.
I take my Old English sheepdog to a groomer who specializes in large **canines.**

compulsory
kəm pul´ sər ē

adj. Required by law or a firm rule.
Training is **compulsory** for all lifeguards.

consecutive
kən sek´ yōo tiv

adj. Following one after another in order.
It rained for five **consecutive** days last week.

desolate
des´ ə lət

adj. 1. Deserted; lonely; without signs of life.
There was not even a gas station on the **desolate** stretch of highway.

2. Filled with sorrow.
The children were **desolate** when the kitten got lost in the woods.

dispatch
di spach´

v. 1. To send on specific business.
The senator **dispatched** an aide to meet with reporters.

2. To finish or complete promptly.
The major **dispatched** the entire plate of oysters before we had tucked in our napkins.

3. To kill quickly.
The rat was **dispatched** with a single blow.

n. (dis´ pach) 1. Speed in movement or performance.
You must act with **dispatch** if you hope to settle the matter by noon tomorrow.

2. A written message sent quickly.
A motorcyclist carried the **dispatches** to the captain.

distinction
di stiŋk´ shən

n. 1. A recognition of the way things differ.
The medical-insurance providers make a **distinction** between temporary and permanent employees.

2. Special honor or regard.
Astronaut John Glenn had the **distinction** of being the first American to orbit Earth.

3. Excellence of performance or ability.
Sarah served as class president with **distinction.**

endure
en door´

v. 1. To put up with; to bear.
The pioneers who headed west had to **endure** incredible hardship along the way.

2. To go on for a long time; to last.
Despite occasional quarrels, my grandparents' marriage **endured** for over fifty years.

endurance   *n.* The ability to put up with hardship; the quality of putting up with hardship.
There is no better test of a runner's **endurance** than the marathon.

fluctuate
fluk´ chōō āt

v. To rise and fall; to keep changing.
The supply of fresh vegetables **fluctuates** with the seasons.

fluctuation   *n.* A rising and falling movement.
In New England, wide temperature **fluctuations** are to be expected in October.

grueling
grōō´ əl iŋ

adj. Tiring; exhausting.
Mt. Washington is a **grueling** climb for most hikers.

maul
môl

v. To handle roughly so as to cause injury.
We chased the cat away before it could **maul** the mouse it had caught.

participate	*v.* To take part in.
pär tis´ ə pāt	The entire class **participated** in the ticket sale for the school musical.
	participant *n.* (pär tis´ ə pənt) One who takes part in.
	All the **participants** in the Thanksgiving Day parade must be in place by 11:00 A.M.
robust	*adj.* Strong and vigorous.
rō bust´	My grandfather is in **robust** health for an eighty-year-old.

19A ▶ Finding Meanings

Choose two phrases to form a sentence that correctly uses a word from Word List 19. Write each sentence in the space provided.

1. (a) that is difficult and exhausting.　(c) that requires much preparation.
   (b) An alternative exercise is one　(d) A grueling exercise is one

   _____

   _____

2. (a) Distinction is　(c) the ability to put up with hardship.
   (b) Endurance is　(d) the ability to understand.

   _____

   _____

3. (a) A desolate road is　(c) one that is presented as a choice.
   (b) An alternative road is　(d) one that is very windy.

   _____

   _____

4. (a) show harm done.　(c) Adverse results
   (b) Fluctuating results　(d) follow one another in proper order.

   _____

   _____

5. (a) A desolate person is one who　(c) is in poor health.
   (b) A robust person is one who　(d) is filled with sorrow.

   _____

   _____

adverse

aloof

alternative

canine

compulsory

consecutive

desolate

dispatch

distinction

endure

fluctuate

grueling

maul

participate

robust

6. (a) To participate is to   (c) act without thinking.
   (b) move up and down.   (d) To fluctuate is to

_____

_____

7. (a) A dispatch is   (c) a quickly sent message.
   (b) a possible course of action.   (d) A distinction is

_____

_____

8. (a) Consecutive tests   (c) Compulsory tests
   (b) fail to show a definite result. (d) follow one another without a break.

_____

_____

9. (a) a member of the dog family.   (c) an injury caused by a bite or scratch.
   (b) A canine is   (d) A participant is

_____

_____

10. (a) An aloof person is one who   (c) stands apart from the rest.
    (b) A robust person is one who   (d) is without hope.

_____

_____

Improve each of the following sentences by crossing out the bold phrase and replacing it with a word (or a form of the word) from Word List 19.

1. The woods are dark and **without a sign of life.**

2. Only persons who are extremely **strong and vigorous** should do these aerobic exercises.

3. Were you one of the **ones taking part** in the 100-meter dash?

4. Wearing seat belts is **required by law** in many states.

5. The trainer was rushed to the hospital when the tiger **attacked him and caused serious injuries to** his left arm and shoulder.

6. The judge **quickly put an end to** the case with an abrupt "These charges should never have been filed."

7. I walked home because the only **other choice open to me** was to wait two hours for the next bus.

8. Did they make any **attempt to show the difference** between what is real and what is imaginary?

9. We learned to **put up with** the long, cold winter season after we moved to Alaska.

10. The reviews were so **negative and damaging** that the play closed in a week.

adverse
aloof
alternative
canine
compulsory
consecutive
desolate
dispatch
distinction
endure
fluctuate
grueling
maul
participate
robust

Circle the letter or letters of each correct answer. A question may have more than one correct answer.

1. Which of the following belongs to the **canine** family?
   (a) a wolf
   (b) a puppy
   (c) a poodle
   (d) a hound

2. In which of the following can anyone **participate?**
   (a) major league baseball
   (b) a recycling program
   (c) July 4th celebrations
   (d) a fund-raising drive

3. Which of the following might show **fluctuations?**
   (a) the price of gasoline
   (b) the demand for oil
   (c) the moon's orbit
   (d) the distance from Seattle to Miami

4. Which of the following run **consecutively?**
   (a) 1999, 2000, 2001
   (b) 9, 11, 12, 10
   (c) May, June, July
   (d) Monday, Wednesday, Friday

5. Which of the following might be described as **desolate?**
   (a) a deserted village
   (b) a congested highway
   (c) a solitary person
   (d) an evicted family

6. Which of the following might be a **grueling** activity?
   (a) running a marathon
   (b) long-distance swimming
   (c) watching a movie
   (d) reading a book

7. Which of the following would be described as **compulsory** in the United States?
   (a) voting in elections
   (b) exercising regularly
   (c) eating balanced meals
   (d) paying any taxes owed

8. Which of the following could be **dispatched?**
   (a) a letter
   (b) a task
   (c) a messenger
   (d) a predatory animal

Each group of four words contains either two synonyms or two antonyms. Circle that pair. Then circle the *S* if they are synonyms or the *A* if they are antonyms.

1. feeble	desolate	beneficial	robust	S	A
2. dispatch	caress	maul	decide	S	A
3. endure	invent	participate	last	S	A
4. excellence	alternative	change	distinction	S	A
5. fluctuation	dispatch	hardiness	speed	S	A
6. joy	wisdom	desolation	fluctuation	S	A
7. friendly	grueling	afraid	aloof	S	A
8. compulsory	advanced	adverse	favorable	S	A
9. option	participant	alternative	hardship	S	A
10. arduous	delicious	grueling	robust	S	A

adverse
aloof
alternative
canine
compulsory
consecutive
desolate
dispatch
distinction
endure
fluctuate
grueling
maul
participate
robust

Read the passage. Then answer the questions that follow it.

The Ultimate Test

Most sports have separate divisions for men and women. No such **distinction** exists between male and female **participants** in the Iditarod, a **grueling** race of sixty or more dogsleds across 1,157 miles from Anchorage to Nome, Alaska. Probably its most famous competitor was Susan Butcher, who won the event for the third **consecutive** year in 1988, and who—despite the most **adverse** weather conditions in the history of the race—went on to win it for a fourth time in 1990. Butcher considered the Iditarod to be the ultimate test of **endurance** for both animals and humans.

The race, which extends over some of the most **desolate** trails on earth, lasts up to fourteen days. The competitors, called "mushers," get little sleep during this time. A **compulsory** twenty-four-hour stopover at the checkpoint of their choice gives them a brief respite. But even the most **robust** mushers have to fight a constant battle with fatigue during the race's final days.

Unpredictable weather conditions are another hazard. Temperatures can **fluctuate** between 50 degrees below zero and 40 degrees above. Snowstorms are not uncommon, with icy winds reaching speeds of 140 miles an hour. In the 1984 race, a section of the overland route was closed. Strong winds had blown away the snow covering. Butcher and her dogs took an **alternative** sea route over the ice-covered Norton Sound. The ice gave way. Susan and her dog team plunged into the frigid water. Led by Granite, her lead dog, they scrambled for shore and went on with the race. Butcher stayed warm by running alongside her sled. That year she came in second.

Wild animals are another of the many dangers mushers face. In the 1985 race, Butcher's dog team was attacked by a starving moose that probably thought her dogs were a pack of wolves. Having to protect her dogs and herself, she fought off the enraged moose with an ax. Finally another musher, who was armed with a gun, pulled up behind her and quickly **dispatched** the moose. Two of her dogs were killed in the attack. Thirteen other dogs were badly **mauled.** That was one year she did not finish.

Born in 1954, Butcher had loved dogs since her youth. In 1975, she moved from her native Cambridge, Massachusetts, to Eureka, Alaska. There she bred and trained dogs at her Trail Breaker Kennels up until her death from leukemia in 2006. As many as 150 dogs were there at any one time. She said that they were all her pets and had the run of her home, although of course not all at once. Butcher was somewhat **aloof** by nature. She was more at ease with her dogs than she was with people. She believed that the secret of her success was the strong bond she formed with her **canine** companions from the time they were born.

▶ **Answer each of the following questions in the form of a sentence. If a question does not contain a vocabulary word from the lesson's word list, use one in your answer. Use each word only once.**

1. What does the phrase "**adverse** weather conditions" suggest?

_____

_____

2. Do temperatures generally remain steady during the course of a race?

_____

_____

3. What are two qualities needed for success in such a **grueling** event?

_____

_____

4. What is the meaning of **desolate** as it is used in the passage?

_____

_____

5. What do the dogsled teams do if the route ahead has no snow?

_____

_____

6. Is the twenty-four-hour stopover voluntary?

_____

_____

7. What is the meaning of **dispatched** as it is used in the passage?

_____

_____

adverse
aloof
alternative
canine
compulsory
consecutive
desolate
dispatch
distinction
endure
fluctuate
grueling
maul
participate
robust

8. Is fatigue a problem during the race's final days?

_____

_____

9. How many of Butcher's dogs were injured when the moose attacked?

_____

_____

10. Why do you think the moose mistook Butcher's dogs for wolves?

_____

_____

11. What does it mean to say that Butcher won for the third **consecutive** year in 1988?

_____

_____

12. Why might the start of the race be particularly hectic?

_____

_____

13. How is the Iditarod different from most athletic contests?

_____

_____

14. Why do you think so many people—like Butcher—respond to the challenge of the Iditarod?

_____

_____

15. Why might Butcher not have enjoyed going to parties?

_____

_____

- **Adverse** should not be confused with *averse*, which means "having an active, strong dislike." If a person has a serious heart condition, strenuous exercise might have an *adverse* effect on that person's health; such a person might, therefore, be *averse* to such exercise.

- Don't confuse **alternative** (the noun or the adjective) with *alternate*, the verb meaning "to happen by turns" or "to take turns." (Boys and girls *alternate* in using the swimming pool.) *Alternate* is also an adjective, meaning "happening by turns" (The wall was painted in *alternate* stripes of red and white) and "every other" (We take turns driving the children on *alternate* days). Finally, *alternate* is a noun meaning "a person chosen to take the place of another." (If you cannot attend the meeting, you must name an *alternate*.)

- **Canine** comes from the Latin word for *dog*, which is *canis*.

  Latin names of other animals provide us with a number of words having to do with animals or with qualities associated with them. Among them are the following: *Apis*, "bee," gives us *apiary*, a collection of hives where bees are kept for their honey. *Avis*, "bird," gives us *aviary*, a large, caged enclosure where birds are kept, and *aviation*, which is the science of airplanes and flying. *Asinus*, "donkey," gives us *asinine*, which means "like a donkey" and hence, "stupid" or "silly" because of the belief that donkeys are stupid animals.

adverse

aloof

alternative

canine

compulsory

consecutive

desolate

dispatch

distinction

endure

fluctuate

grueling

maul

participate

robust

Lesson **20**

For more practice and games, go to **www.WordlyWise3000.com**.

| Word List | Study the definitions of the words. Then do the exercises that follow. |

apathy
ap´ ə thē

n. A lack of interest or concern.
The low turnout in local elections is the result of the **apathy** of the citizens.

apathetic   *adj.* (ap ə thet´ ik) Unconcerned; uninterested.
Some teenagers remain **apathetic** about politics until they can vote.

badger
baj´ ər

v. To keep bothering.
Reporters **badgered** the mayor to provide details of the plan for the new library.

n. A strongly built, burrowing mammal common in many northern parts of the world.
The European **badger** weighs up to thirty pounds and is somewhat larger than its North American counterpart.

compel
kəm pel´

v. To force or require to do something.
A strong sense of duty **compels** firefighters to risk their lives.

delude
də lōōd´

v. To mislead; to deceive.
Despite negative messages from the polls, the candidate **deluded** himself into thinking he could win.

delusion   *n.* (də lōō´ zhən) A false or mistaken belief.
His belief that he is Napoleon is a **delusion.**

deplore
di plôr´

v. 1. To feel or express sorrow or regret.
My father **deplored** the fact that he hadn't spent more time with his children when they were young.

2. To disapprove of strongly.
Upper levels of management **deplored** the loss of middle-management jobs as the corporation down-sized.

deplorable   *adj.* Very bad; wretched.
Living conditions in the Warsaw ghetto were **deplorable.**

derelict
der´ ə likt

adj. 1. Dilapidated and abandoned.
The **derelict** building will be torn down soon.

2. Lacking a sense of duty; neglectful.
The supervisor was **derelict** in not having the repairs inspected.

n. A poor, homeless person.
The plan will help **derelicts** by providing shelters and assisting them in finding gainful employment.

detriment
de´ trə mənt

n. 1. Damage or harm.
She willingly stayed home with her young children to the **detriment** of her career.

2. Anything that causes harm.
Tobacco is a **detriment** to the health of smokers.

detrimental *adj.* Damaging; harmful.
Eating too much "junk food" is **detrimental** to one's health.

diversity
də vʉr´ sə tē

n. 1. The condition of being different or having differences.
I was struck by the **diversity** in the personalities of the twins.

2. Variety.
The library offers a great **diversity** of materials on local history.

emit
ē mit´

v. 1. To give off or send out.
A candle **emits** very little light.

2. To utter or express.
The cat **emitted** a loud screech when I accidentally stepped on its tail.

emission *n.* (ē mish´ ən) Something that is emitted.
Carbon monoxide is an odorless yet deadly **emission** from engine exhausts.

foster
fôs´ tər

v. To promote the growth of; to encourage.
The music teacher **fostered** an interest in jazz in his students.

adj. Giving or receiving care in a family that is not related by birth or adoption.
The Becks are **foster** parents to three small children.

inanimate
in an´ ə mət

adj. Lacking qualities associated with living things.
A stone is an **inanimate** object.

incentive
in sen´ tiv

n. Something that makes a person want to try or work harder.
A local benefactor offers $1,000 scholarships as an **incentive** to students to stay in school.

omen
ō´ mən

n. An event or sign that is believed to indicate the future.
Do you believe that a black cat is an **omen** of bad luck?

ominous *adj.* (äm´ ə nəs) Of or like a bad omen; threatening.
An **ominous** silence greeted us when we entered the room.

species
spē´ shēz

n. A group of plants or animals that are similar in some ways.
There are over a million different **species** of beetle in the world.

toxic
täks´ ik

adj. Causing harm; poisonous.
Pokeweed can be **toxic** to birds that eat its seeds.

Choose two phrases to form a sentence that correctly uses a word from Word List 20. Write each sentence in the space provided.

1. (a) one who is not actually related to a child.
   (b) A foster parent is
   (c) one who expresses interest in a child.
   (d) A derelict parent is

   _____

   _____

2. (a) A species is
   (b) An omen is
   (c) a clear choice between alternatives.
   (d) a group of similar plants or animals.

   _____

   _____

3. (a) the state of being confused.
   (b) Diversity is
   (c) Apathy is
   (d) the condition of having differences.

   _____

   _____

4. (a) a poor, homeless person.
   (b) A derelict is
   (c) A badger is
   (d) something that is unexplained.

   _____

   _____

5. (a) causes one to work harder.
   (b) An incentive is something that
   (c) A delusion is something that
   (d) causes injury or damage.

   _____

   _____

6. (a) Detriment is
   (b) Apathy is
   (c) a lack of interest or concern.
   (d) material for which there is no use.

   _____

   _____

7. (a) something that has been left out.
   (b) a strongly held but false belief.
   (c) A delusion is
   (d) An emission is

   _____

   _____

8. (a) To deplore change is
   (b) to study it.
   (c) To compel change is
   (d) to disapprove of it.

   _____

   _____

9. (a) An inanimate object is
   (b) one that causes harm.
   (c) one that arouses interest or curiosity.
   (d) A detrimental object is

   _____

   _____

10. (a) An emission is
    (b) A badger is
    (c) something held back.
    (d) something given off.

    _____

    _____

20B · Just the Right Word

Improve each of the following sentences by crossing out the bold phrase and replacing it with a word (or a form of the word) from Word List 20.

1. The amanita mushroom is **likely to cause illness or death** if eaten.

2. The object we examined under the microscope appeared to be **without any of the qualities associated with living things.**

3. A red sky at night is believed to be an **indication that gives the promise** of good weather.

4. The children **kept on bothering** me until I agreed to take them to the circus.

5. The candidate was **misled by his mistaken beliefs** into thinking that the local newspaper would endorse him for Congress.

6. The *Voyager* space probe continued to **give off** signals from deep space.

7. The mayor **expressed regret about** the lack of funds for inner-city schools.

8. When it is brought up today, the subject of homeschooling produces a great **number of differences** of opinion.

9. You are not **required or forced** to give evidence against yourself in court.

10. The United Nations tries to **promote the growth of** greater understanding between countries.

apathy
badger
compel
delude
deplore
derelict
detriment
diversity
emit
foster
inanimate
incentive
omen
species
toxic

Circle the letter or letters of each correct answer. A question may have more than one correct answer.

1. Which of the following are **detrimental** to good health?
   (a) exercising
   (b) working
   (c) resting
   (d) overeating

2. Which of the following can **foster** education?
   (a) parents
   (b) libraries
   (c) teachers
   (d) experiences

3. Which of the following might result from an **incentive?**
   (a) working harder
   (b) working longer
   (c) working indifferently
   (d) working heedlessly

4. Which of the following sounds **ominous?**
   (a) a lucrative offer
   (b) a distraught cry
   (c) an eerie moan
   (d) an allegation of negligence

5. Which of the following are members of a **species?**
   (a) human beings
   (b) planets
   (c) menageries
   (d) bald eagles

6. Which of the following might a person **deplore?**
   (a) a blatant lie
   (b) an intrepid act
   (c) an angry retort
   (d) a momentous discovery

7. Which of the following might describe an **apathetic** person?
   (a) industrious
   (b) lethargic
   (c) agitated
   (d) exuberant

8. Which of the following can be **emitted?**
   (a) smoke
   (b) a cry
   (c) a signal
   (d) a ray of light

Complete the analogies by selecting the pair of words whose relationship most resembles the relationship of the pair in capital letters. Circle the letter of the pair you choose.

1. INANIMATE : LIFE ::
   (a) lethargic : energy
   (b) apathetic : boredom
   (c) robust : health
   (d) perturbed : fear

2. BADGER : MAMMAL ::
   (a) plant : animal
   (b) finger : hand
   (c) hammer : saw
   (d) rattlesnake : reptile

3. DETRIMENTAL : BENEFICIAL ::
   (a) intrepid : brave
   (b) tedious : boring
   (c) difficult : grueling
   (d) fragile : robust

4. BIGOTRY : TOLERANCE ::
   (a) sovereign : monarch
   (b) bleakness : hope
   (c) insulation : warmth
   (d) ghetto : poverty

5. REFUSE : SPURN ::
   (a) eat : drink
   (b) sleep : wake
   (c) annoy : harass
   (d) procure : obtain

6. ACTUAL : PROSPECTIVE ::
   (a) obvious : subtle
   (b) sleek : mottled
   (c) trifling : significant
   (d) present : future

7. APATHY : CONCERN ::
   (a) variety : diversity
   (b) lethargy : energy
   (c) theme : topic
   (d) acclaim : praise

8. EMIT : ABSORB ::
   (a) covet : envy
   (b) emerge : submerge
   (c) maul : harm
   (d) spurn : reject

9. EBB : FLOW ::
   (a) vary : fluctuate
   (b) end : terminate
   (c) recede : advance
   (d) perturb : disturb

10. ASSENT : ASCENT ::
    (a) sleek : slick
    (b) deny : admit
    (c) fluster : foster
    (d) pique : peek

apathy
badger
compel
delude
deplore
derelict
detriment
diversity
emit
foster
inanimate
incentive
omen
species
toxic

Read the passage. Then answer the questions that follow it.

Saving the Planet

Smog is a mixture of smoke and fog. Americans became unhappily aware of it in the 1960s when it hung over Los Angeles for days on end. Smog made the air not only unpleasant to breathe but actually **detrimental** to people's health. Many believed this polluted air, produced by smoke from vehicle exhausts and factory chimneys, to be an **omen** of things to come if people did not take better care of the environment.

The environment is the world we inhabit—everything living and **inanimate.** Environmentalists are people who wish to preserve the environment; they **deplore** the damage we are doing to it. They remind us that we share our planet with an estimated thirty million or so other **species** of plants and animals. They cherish this **diversity** of life and believe we all should.

For a long time, governments, both at the state and national level, had been **derelict** when it came to protecting the environment. The chief reason for this was the **apathy** of the public. The public was largely unaware of environmental damage until it was almost too late. Rachel Carson's *Silent Spring*, published in 1962, warned of the harm being done to the environment by overuse of chemical fertilizers and pesticides. Her book had an enormous impact. Voters began to take an interest in environmental issues. That gave lawmakers the **incentive** to take action. Environmentalists **badgered** Congress to pass laws such as the Clean Air Acts of 1970 and 1990. Finally, industries that were the worst polluters were **compelled** to reduce the **emissions** from vehicles and factory chimneys.

Citizens cannot, however, be **deluded** into thinking that simply passing laws will protect people from environmental harm. Individuals must remain active. An example of a person who did just this is Janice Dickerson. She made it her mission in life to educate people about the dangers of living along a seventy-five-mile stretch of the Mississippi River south of Baton Rouge, Louisiana. During recent decades, it witnessed the building of more than one hundred chemical factories and oil refineries. Those factories emitted smoke from chimneys and dumped chemicals into the river. Known as "cancer alley," this area has one of the highest cancer rates in the United States.

Lois Gibbs is another person active in the environmental movement. In 1978, it was discovered that Love Canal, three blocks from her home near Buffalo, New York, had been a dumping ground for **toxic** chemicals. The local residents feared that they too would suffer from the asthma and blood disorders experienced by some of their neighbors. They felt forced to abandon their homes. Gibbs moved to Washington, D.C., where she runs a consulting service for people across the country who find themselves in situations similar to that of the people of Love Canal. She also speaks about such issues across the country.

One of the most effective ways of getting people involved in environmental issues has been Earth Day. The purpose of Earth Day is to **foster** awareness of the harm we are doing to our planet. Started in 1970 in the United States, it has grown rapidly, and on Earth Day 2009, more than a billion people around the world participated in its activities. Earth Day is celebrated each year on April 22, but to those who care about the environment, every day is Earth Day.

▶ **Answer each of the following questions in the form of a sentence. If a question does not contain a vocabulary word from the lesson's word list, use one in your answer. Use each word only once.**

1. Is the environment composed only of living things?

_____

_____

2. How might your class **foster** awareness of Earth Day?

_____

_____

3. Why was it necessary to reduce smog in the nation's cities?

_____

_____

4. In terms of their future, what did people especially fear about smog?

_____

_____

5. Why did people have to abandon their homes near Love Canal?

_____

_____

apathy
badger
compel
delude
deplore
derelict
detriment
diversity
emit
foster
inanimate
incentive
omen
species
toxic

6. Were Dickerson and Gibbs content simply to **deplore** the harm being done to the environment?

_____

_____

7. How did Rachel Carson help to end people's **apathy?**

_____

_____

8. What is the meaning of **derelict** as it is used in the passage?

_____

_____

9. Why did lawmakers wait until 1970 to pass the first Clean Air Act?

_____

_____

10. How did environmentalists influence Congress to do something about pollution?

_____

_____

11. What effect did laws such as the Clean Air Acts have on industry?

_____

_____

12. What was the main cause of the smog in Los Angeles in the 1960s?

_____

_____

13. What might you say about someone who claims that the environment is unharmed?

_____

_____

14. What does every human being have in common with every other human?

_____

_____

15. Why do environmentalists wish to preserve the environment?

_____

_____

- The Greek word *pathos* means "suffering" or "feeling" and has passed unchanged into English; *pathos* in English means "something that moves a person to feel pity." The Greek prefix *ab-* (sometimes written *a-*) means "not" or "without" and combines with *pathos* to form the word **apathy.** A person who cannot feel for others or who doesn't care about them is in a state of *apathy*. We say that such a person is *apathetic*.

  The Greek prefix *syn-* (sometimes written *sym-*) means "with" or "together." It combines with *pathos* to form the noun *sympathy,* "an emotional feeling for other people and a sharing of their sorrow." The adjective form is *sympathetic.* If you have a serious problem, you need to talk to someone who is *sympathetic.* Someone who is *apathetic* would not be interested in your problem.

- Don't confuse **emit,** which means "to give off," with *omit,* which means "to leave out."

- **Species** is both a singular noun (a *species*) and a plural noun (many *species*). A species is one of the major groups into which all living things—plants and animals—are divided. Although the production of offspring normally takes place only within the same species, creatures of different, though related, species can produce offspring. An example of this is the mule; it is the result of mating a male donkey with a female horse.

  Specie (a less common word, spelled without the final *s*) means "money in the form of coin." Dollar bills are paper money. Nickels, dimes, and quarters are money in the form of *specie.*

apathy
badger
compel
delude
deplore
derelict
detriment
diversity
emit
foster
inanimate
incentive
omen
species
toxic

Hidden Message   In the boxes provided, write the words from Lessons 17 through 20 that are missing in each of the sentences. The number following each sentence gives the word list from which the missing word is taken. When the exercise is finished, the shaded boxes should spell out a Burma Shave jingle. From the 1920s to the 1960s, Burma Shave signs—a form of advertising for a shaving cream—were a familiar sight on American roads. On four or five regularly spaced signs, short messages were spelled out for travelers to read as they passed by. This one dates back to 1949.

1. Grain prices _____ greatly from year to year. **(19)**

2. The play's _____ is the healing power of love. **(18)**

3. Her parents admire their _____ son-in-law. **(18)**

4. I was surprised to hear him _____ such a generous offer. **(18)**

5. That row of _____ houses is to be torn down. **(20)**

6. I am a _____ supporter of the right to free speech. **(18)**

7. You might have to _____ to get a lower price. **(17)**

8. A _____ country will not allow foreign interference. **(17)**

9. She continues to _____ herself into thinking that the job will be easy. **(20)**

10. The child was placed in the care of _____ parents. **(20)**

11. I think the company will be _____ to my offer. **(17)**

12. The _____ of plant life in the rain forest is enormous. **(20)**

13. The last five miles of the marathon were _____. **(19)**

14. Why _____ the possessions of others? **(18)**

15. The curfew will _____ youths to be home by 1 a.m. **(20)**

16. You give your _____ to the proposal by voting yes. **(17)**

17. Some mushrooms are _____, so they shouldn't be eaten. **(20)**

18. If you bother it, the bear may _____ you. **(19)**

19. The members _____ with our decision to raise the dues. **(17)**

20. I tried to _____ her from leaving school. **(17)**

21. The family felt trapped in the inner city _____. **(18)**

22. A _____ handler looks after the dogs. **(19)**

23. We want everyone to _____ in the project. **(19)**

24. It rained last month for twelve _____ days. **(19)**

25. Raising a sunken ship is a _____ task. **(18)**

26. An honest person will _____ a bribe. **(17)**

27. Acid rain has an _____ affect on plant growth. **(19)**

28. She has the _____ of winning two Nobel prizes. **(19)**

29. Stars _____ light and other forms of energy. **(20)**

30. The _____ left a wife and one grown child. **(18)**

31. I do not _____ any difference between them. **(18)**

32. He preferred to stay _____ from the crowd. **(19)**

33. It is _____ to register your car in all states. **(19)**

34. I managed to _____ some extra supplies. **(17)**

35. His continued absence began to _____ me. **(17)**

36. It is in the nature of dictators to _____ the people. **(18)**

37. Even at ninety, her health remained _____. **(19)**

38. Some people don't vote because of _____. **(20)**

39. The medical breakthrough won national _____. **(18)**

40. They'll _____ him until he changes his mind. **(20)**

41. The music of Mozart will _____ forever. **(19)**

42. The _____ of their neighbors made the newcomers uncomfortable. **(18)**

43. Rocks, cars, and planets are all _____ objects. **(20)**

44. We _____ violence in all its forms. **(20)**

45. There is an _____ route into town. **(19)**

46. Lions and tigers belong to different _____. **(20)**

47. The president _____ federal judges. **(17)**

48. Smoking is _____ to one's health. **(20)**

49. The _____ of her new play is tomorrow night. **(18)**

50. Antarctica is the most _____ place on earth. **(19)**

51. The + sign is used to _____ addition. **(17)**

52. We will _____ a repair crew at once to fix the fault. **(19)**

53. A red sunset is an _____ of good weather. **(20)**

54. The fall of Rome was a _____ event in world history. **(18)**

55. You should _____ your doctor if the pain worsens. **(17)**

56. Joining the orchestra was her _____ for practicing so many hours. **(20)**

Pronunciation Key

Symbol	Key Words	Symbol	Key Words
a	c**a**t	b	**b**ed
ā	**a**pe	d	**d**og
ä	c**o**t, c**ar**	f	**f**all
â	be**ar**	g	**g**et
		h	**h**elp
e	t**e**n, b**e**rry	j	**j**ump
ē	m**e**	k	**k**iss, **c**all
		l	**l**eg, bott**l**e
i	f**i**t	m	**m**eat
ī	**i**ce, f**i**re	n	**n**ose, kitte**n**
		p	**p**ut
ō	g**o**	r	**r**ed
ô	f**a**ll, f**or**	s	**s**ee
oi	**oi**l	t	**t**op
σο	l**oo**k, p**u**ll	v	**v**at
ōō	t**oo**l, r**u**le	w	**w**ish
ou	**o**ut, cr**o**wd	y	**y**ard
		z	**z**ebra
u	**u**p		
ʉ	f**u**r, sh**i**rt	ch	**ch**in, ar**ch**
		ŋ	ri**ng**, dri**n**k
ə	**a** in **a**go	sh	**sh**e, pu**sh**
	e in ag**e**nt	th	**th**in, tru**th**
	i in penc**i**l	*th*	**th**en, fa**th**er
	o in at**o**m	zh	mea**s**ure
	u in circ**u**s		
´	hospital (häs´ pit'l)		

A stress mark ´ is placed after a syllable that gets a primary stress, as in **vocabulary** (vō kab´ yə ler ē).